Cambridge Elements ≡

Elements in the Politics of Development
edited by
Melani Cammett
Harvard University
Ben Ross Schneider
Massachusetts Institute of Technology

Series co-sponsored by

 MIT CENTER FOR INTERNATIONAL STUDIES

COERCIVE DISTRIBUTION

Michael Albertus
University of Chicago

Sofia Fenner
Bryn Mawr College, Pennsylvania

Dan Slater
University of Michigan, Ann Arbor

CAMBRIDGE
UNIVERSITY PRESS

University Printing House, Cambridge CB2 8BS, United Kingdom

One Liberty Plaza, 20th Floor, New York, NY 10006, USA

477 Williamstown Road, Port Melbourne, VIC 3207, Australia

314–321, 3rd Floor, Plot 3, Splendor Forum, Jasola District Centre,
New Delhi – 110025, India

79 Anson Road, #06–04/06, Singapore 079906

Cambridge University Press is part of the University of Cambridge.

It furthers the University's mission by disseminating knowledge in the pursuit of
education, learning, and research at the highest international levels of excellence.

www.cambridge.org
Information on this title: www.cambridge.org/9781108462136
DOI: 10.1017/9781108644334

© Michael Albertus, Sofia Fenner, and Dan Slater 2018

First published 2018

A catalogue record for this publication is available from the British Library.

ISBN 978-1-108-46213-6 Paperback
ISSN 2515-1584 (online)
ISSN 2515-1576 (print)

Coercive Distribution

Michael Albertus, Sofia Fenner, and Dan Slater

Abstract: *Canonical theories of political economy struggle to explain patterns of distribution in authoritarian regimes. In this Element, Albertus, Fenner, and Slater challenge existing models and introduce an alternative, supply-side, and state-centered theory of "coercive distribution." Authoritarian regimes proactively deploy distributive policies as advantageous strategies to consolidate their monopoly on power. These policies contribute to authoritarian durability by undercutting rival elites and enmeshing the masses in lasting relations of coercive dependence. The authors illustrate the patterns, timing, and breadth of coercive distribution with global and Latin American quantitative evidence and with a series of historical case studies from regimes in Latin America, Asia, and the Middle East. By recognizing distribution's coercive dimensions, they account for empirical patterns of distribution that do not fit with quasi-democratic understandings of distribution as quid pro quo exchange. Under authoritarian conditions, distribution is less an alternative to coercion than one of its most effective expressions.*

Keywords: *authoritarianism, distribution, coercion, clientelism, land reform*

ISSNs: *2515-1584 (online), 2515-1576 (print)*

ISBNs: *9781108462136 (PB), 9781108644334 (OC)*

Introduction

Some of the world's most distributive regimes have been authoritarian. From Mexico to Malaysia, from Cuba to China, and from Tanzania to Taiwan, authoritarian rulers have embarked upon massive distributive programs,[1] extending housing, education, basic services, jobs, and land to some of their poorest citizens – often at the expense of economic elites. This empirical record stands in sharp contrast to dominant theories of authoritarian political economy, which suggest that nondemocratic regimes should distribute narrowly, if at all. Such models struggle to account for authoritarian regimes that distribute broadly or to groups beyond their closest allies. By conceptualizing distributive politics in authoritarian regimes as a quid pro quo exchange of economic benefits for political support, scholars have created an important puzzle: why would authoritarian regimes distribute scarce resources to impoverished and marginalized citizens, even when those citizens lack the collective capacity to demand them?

We answer this question by highlighting authoritarianism's coercive foundations. This requires attentiveness to the power differential between state-based distributors and society-based recipients under authoritarian conditions. Our supply-side, state-centered theory argues that comprehensive distributive programs are an advantageous way for young authoritarian regimes to confront both elite and mass threats. At the elite level, extending distributive programs displaces rival service providers and undermines the position of preexisting elites who might threaten a new regime's consolidation of power. At the mass level, comprehensive distribution has the great authoritarian virtue of cultivating dependence and curtailing subjects' exit options. When ordinary citizens depend upon an authoritarian-run state rather than rival, nonstate providers for their basic material necessities, their ability to individually defy or collectively mobilize against their rulers is severely compromised.

Broad distribution, then, can help authoritarian regimes sideline rival elites and facilitate mass control. It contributes to regime stability not by "buying off" threatening actors or rewarding

---

[1] Distribution to the poor does not necessarily require extraction from the rich, as our cases demonstrate. Our core puzzle is not why authoritarian regimes extract from wealthy elites, but why they devote scarce economic resources to the poor and (at least on average) the powerless.

staunch supporters but by undercutting rivals and enmeshing citizens in relationships of dependence. Hence, we refer to such comprehensive distributive programs under authoritarian conditions as *coercive distribution*. In doing so, we highlight the ways in which distribution – so often considered as an alternative to repression – can, in fact, be one of its most effective expressions.

Coercive distribution is common, but it is neither universal nor uniform. Many authoritarian regimes do not pursue it at all, and those that do may do so to different extents and with varying degrees of political commitment over time. Our global and especially Latin American quantitative evidence as well as our historical case studies show that coercive distribution takes place in three major phases: *displacement* of rival elites, *enmeshment* of citizens in relations of dependence, and trajectories of *upkeep*. Not all cases feature all three phases. But the phases of displacement, enmeshment, and upkeep are recurrent enough that we organize our empirical material in the following sections primarily according to these three phases.

We begin by addressing the question of coercive distribution's origins. Why does it characterize some authoritarian political economies but not others? The main reason coercive distribution arises, we argue, is elite splits. More specifically, we emphasize the fundamental significance of coalitional splits between ruling political elites and aristocratic elites with alternative sources of social control. Such aristocratic elites most commonly base their wealth and social control on the ownership of land, though they may draw on other sources, including trade. To the extent that rulers closely ally with aristocratic and landed elites, coercive distribution is unlikely to gather steam, despite its general strategic benefits for durability-seeking autocrats. Coercive distribution typically commences with the quick hammer blow of elite displacement, and it is prior elite splits that best explain why newborn authoritarian regimes consider it necessary to go on the immediate offensive against their elite rivals.[2]

---

[2] Elite splits have a complex relationship with a second (and secondary) causal factor at the origin point of coercive distribution: leftist ideology. It is no

Elite displacement is only the first (and fastest) phase of coercive distribution. It is followed by the enactment and implementation of far-reaching distributive policies that deliver basic necessities to the vast majority of the populace, appropriating the social role of now-displaced rival elites. We call this second phase *enmeshment*. Although many distributive policies can enmesh the masses in relations of coercive dependence, we place special stress on land reform as an important way in which authoritarian regimes can secure quiescence by making ordinary subjects dependent on state authorities instead of landed elites for their "strategies of survival" (Migdal 1988). If an authoritarian regime is to enmesh its citizenry in deeply dependent relationships over the long haul, it must not only build up state infrastructure for public provision. It must also commit to the *upkeep* of that infrastructure over time, including the relatively generous financing of spending programs as both populations and neoliberal pressures for balanced budgets inexorably increase.

Why do some authoritarian regimes succeed more than others at the challenging downstream tasks of enmeshment and upkeep? Although we do not purport to provide a general answer to this causal question here, our analysis centers on state capacity. Whether due to colonial inheritance, the pressures of internal or external warfare, or other more contingent factors, some postcolonial authoritarian regimes enjoy access to much stronger state apparatuses than others. These infrastructural Leviathans provide ideal vehicles for authoritarian rulers to establish and maintain

coincidence that coercive distribution became globally common during the Cold War, as socialist ideals spread across the developing world. Adamantly leftist regimes such as those in China and Cuba were forerunners at coercive distribution, and there is no reason to doubt the importance of deeply felt ideological commitments in galvanizing broad-based distribution in such cases. Yet it is difficult to disentangle leftist ideology from the elite splits that inevitably accompanied it. Since we locate numerous examples in the following sections of anti-socialist regimes that pursued coercive distribution, we place our primary emphasis on the elite splits that characterized virtually all of our cases, instead of the leftist ideology witnessed in only a subset of them.

coercive control over the masses through monopolistic manipulation of downward economic distribution.

Our analysis is organized as follows: the first section begins by surveying the literature on authoritarian distribution, which intersects with broader literatures on public goods provision and the political economy of regimes. We separate existing accounts into five "models": punishment regime, squeaky wheel, co-optation, performance legitimacy, and winning coalition. We then lay out our own model, coercive distribution, as an alternative. Section 2 uses empirics drawn from Latin America and around the world to demonstrate that existing models fail to account for actual patterns of distribution – and that coercive distribution can better explain empirical realities. The discussion is organized chronologically in three sections, corresponding to coercive distribution's three phases: displacement of rival elites, enmeshment of citizens, and trajectories of upkeep and decay. At the same time, each section offers case studies that are grouped regionally (Asia, Latin America, and the Middle East).

Not every country appears in every section, however, and not all three phases receive equal attention. For reasons that we theorize, some regimes have been able to implement enmeshment without displacement, and we do not trace the trajectories of every case up to the present. Furthermore, the upkeep phase receives less attention than the phases of displacement and enmeshment, for two main reasons. First, this final phase is least important for establishing our core argument that distributive policies in authoritarian regimes arise through a coercive rather than contractual logic. Second, upkeep is almost certainly explained by different factors than the elite splits that best explain displacement and the state capacity that underpins successful enmeshment. Doing justice to the dynamics of upkeep would require another sort of analysis, as we briefly discuss in the Conclusion.

As for the case studies, we have selected a range of cases in which the availability of historical data and the unfolding of country-level processes have rendered the mechanisms of coercive distribution especially visible. Through causal process observations within each case study, we pit coercive distribution against alternative models of authoritarian distribution endemic to specific regional literatures: for example, clientelism and co-optation in the Middle East, performance legitimacy in Asia, and selectorate theory and squeaky wheel explanations in Latin America.

1 Theory and Argument

The question of why authoritarian rulers distribute resources to their subjects remains a persistent puzzle in the literature on non-democratic regimes. In democratic contexts, voter preferences and interest group pressures are assumed to determine the distribution of resources; the imperative to appease the median voter is supposed to produce broad distribution that roughly resembles the provision of public goods (see, e.g., Meltzer and Richard 1981; Persson and Tabellini 2002).[3] At first glance, authoritarian regimes seem comparatively free from such pressures. Yet while some nondemocratic regimes do indeed make few gestures toward downward distribution, others embark upon comprehensive programs of service provision. To explain this seemingly puzzling outcome, scholars usually conceptualize distributive authoritarian regimes as quasi-democracies, focusing on how distribution serves aims of cultivating political support by endearing citizens and/or powerful elites to their rulers.[4]

---

[3] Of course, democracies can and do deviate from these predictions for a host of reasons ranging from group consciousness and cross-cutting cleavages to place-based identity and priming or framing effects (see Bartels 2005; Roemer 1998; Shapiro 2002; Walsh 2012). Furthermore, political representatives may have a greater stake in translating the demands of some voters over those of others (Atkinson 2015; Gilens and Page 2014).

[4] To be clear, the problem is not a failure to recognize authoritarian actions such as coercion and repression. Rather, it is the assumption that while some authoritarian acts may be repressive, others are simply geared toward encouraging subjects to support incumbent regimes – a practice endemic to democracies. This assumption obscures the possibility that policies that seem geared toward *attracting* supporters may in fact be working to *control* them.

Our approach is different: we explain patterns of authoritarian distribution by taking authoritarianism seriously as an undemocratic system of rule – one predicated not on the credible promise of mutually beneficial exchange but instead on the credible threat of unidirectional force. In this section, we explain why such a new approach is needed: existing theories fail to account for observable patterns of authoritarian distribution. In particular, we find that these theories have particular difficulty explaining comprehensive distributive programs that reach both supporters and opponents of a regime. These programs are of enormous political importance: not only have they fundamentally impacted billions of lives, but they also have paved the way for some of the longest-lived authoritarian regimes of the twentieth and twenty-first centuries.

1.1 Existing Models of Authoritarian Distribution

We group extant accounts into five logics of authoritarian distribution. We call these winning coalition, squeaky wheel, co-optation, punishment regime, and performance legitimacy (see Table 1 for a graphical representation). None of these models, we suggest, can adequately account for those authoritarian regimes that undertake broad distributive policies.

Winning coalition models dominate current studies of authoritarian political economy. Based in selectorate theory (Bueno de Mesquita et al., 2003; Morrow et al. 2008), they tend to predict that authoritarian regimes will distribute only to an exclusive coterie of elites or a specific ethnic constituency. In short, autocracy will look like kleptocracy (i.e., a system of narrow distribution to regime cronies) or ethnocracy (i.e., a system of targeted distribution to co-ethnics). Moreover, selectorate theory minimizes the structural differences between authoritarian and democratic regimes by effectively reimagining authoritarian regimes as democracies

Authoritarian institutions ultimately serve not to appease citizens but to ensure subjects' acquiescence, not to expand access to power but to limit it.

Table 1 Models of Authoritarian Distribution

Coerciveness of Distribution	Breadth of Distribution	
	Comprehensive	Targeted
More Coercive	Coercive Distribution	Punishment Regime
Less Coercive	Performance Legitimacy	Clientelism (vote buying, "competitive clientelism," side payments)
	Selectorate Theory (W/S is large; comprehensive goods provision as efficient shortcut)	Selectorate Theory (W/S is small) Kleptocracy/Cronyism (breadth contingent on size of ruling clique) Ethnocracy (breadth contingent on size of ruling clique)

with highly limited selectorates. When authoritarian rulers distribute resources, they appear to be acting no differently from their democratic counterparts: peacefully assembling a "winning coalition" of supporters to remain in power.

Bueno de Mesquita et al. (2003) posit that the size of the winning coalition (W), in particular the relationship of W to the total set of people who have the legal authority to choose political leaders (the selectorate, or S), is a key determinant of how broadly regimes will distribute. Where W/S is small, as in authoritarian regimes with elections (Bueno de Mesquita et al. 2003, 68), distribution will be limited and focused on providing private goods to cronies. Where W/S is large, as in electoral democracies, distribution will look much more like the provision of public goods (ibid. 130).[5]

---

[5] This opens the door for selectorate theory to explain authoritarian goods in principle, but in practice a key methodological problem emerges: W is not identifiable a priori. Without knowing anything about patterns of distribution,

However, in many cases we observe authoritarian distribution that clearly exceeds the boundaries of any plausible winning coalition. In Taiwan, Singapore, and Mexico – to take just a few examples under consideration here – authoritarian regimes have historically held regular, unfair elections. Electoral authoritarian regimes have a small W/S ratio, which should – according to selectorate theory – produce cronyism, not broad distribution. Yet broad distribution has been a surprisingly common result. In Mexico under the Partido Revolucionario Institucional (PRI), for instance, more than half of all land in the country was doled out to villages in communal *ejidos*. In Singapore under the People's Action Party (PAP), more than 90 percent of the population has been provided with public housing.

Squeaky wheel arguments import a democratic logic of societal demand and governmental response into authoritarian contexts. This logic predicts distribution toward those communities or groups that make public claims on regime resources, whether they are peasants mobilizing for development assistance or urbanites demanding better schools. As Wallace puts it in his analysis of authoritarian distribution in China, "the squeaky wheel gets the grease" (2014: 35). Squeaky wheel arguments are compatible with distribution toward actors who are not necessarily supportive of the regime. If those making noise are not supporters, they may still receive benefits. Like their selectorate counterparts, however, squeaky wheel arguments struggle to account for *comprehensive* distribution: it is unlikely that all of society will equally and actively clamor for distribution, especially under authoritarianism's repressive conditions.

Moreover, squeaky wheel arguments also require careful causal process observations to avoid sinking into tautology. For such claims to be convincing, scholars must demonstrate actual public claim making by citizens prior to and consistent with subsequent

a scholar cannot determine whether any given actor is a member of a winning coalition. This makes selectorate theory explanations difficult to falsify, since measurements of winning coalition size are often read from patterns of distribution, rather than being used to predict them.

authoritarian distribution and not infer citizens' demands from their receipt of resources. In the case studies we present, minimal public claim making preceded distribution; in some cases, peasant communities that received benefits barely recognized the central state, let alone demanded that it provide them with land or the resources necessary to cultivate it.

The logic of *co-optation,* similarly, predicts that regimes will distribute toward those actors or groups that pose a potential threat to regime survival, thus ensuring their loyalty – or at least quiescence – via material payoffs. In recent years, the notion of co-optation as institutional inclusion has been replaced with a concept of co-optation as benefit provision (e.g., Gandhi and Przeworski 2007; Svolik 2012). It has thus become a commonplace in studies of authoritarianism that potential opponents can usually be bought off if a ruler can find the right price. Much like their squeaky wheel counterparts, convincing co-optation arguments must establish that (1) groups that receive benefits actually are understood as potential threats by the regime, (2) benefits really are changing hands, and (3) co-optative buyoffs actually work to neutralize opponents (Fenner 2016). In many of the cases we consider, such evidence is lacking.

Punishment regime theories (the term is Magaloni's [2006]) come closest to taking the coercive side of authoritarian distribution seriously. In these accounts, rulers distribute resources to those who support them and withhold resources from those who do not. This logic emphasizes a politics of reciprocal exchange in which political support is offered conditionally in return for essentially simultaneous resource disbursements. Authoritarian elections, and the political parties that come with them, are often understood as key components of punishment regime theories, since they give rulers information about constituency- and individual-level loyalties and provide arenas and occasions for targeted distribution.

Scholars of clientelism have also recognized the repressive dimensions of punishment regime practices. As Stokes et al. write of certain clientelistic arrangements, "an implicit threat to cut a voter off from future benefits as a direct result of his or her voting choices moves uncomfortably close to coercion" (2013: 13). Still, in punishment regime and most clientelist models, citizens exchange their political support for desired or needed goods, and resource flows go only to supporters. One segment of the population complies and receives carrots; the other part resists and gets the stick. These models remain unable to account for comprehensive distributive programs, which reach supporters and opponents alike.

Finally, *performance legitimacy* models suggest that authoritarian regimes will benefit from greater popular support if they provide high-quality infrastructure, rising incomes, and steady economic growth. Such arguments are clearly compatible with broad distribution, since the benefits in question work because they reach all citizens indiscriminately, purchasing quiescence among the otherwise dissatisfied and active support among the otherwise neutral.

Performance legitimacy logics, however, leave several key questions unanswered. If we understand legitimacy as popular support and set aside methodological problems related to observing sincerity (see Wedeen 1999), then it is certainly true that democratic incumbents need legitimacy, at least in relative terms, to survive in power. Many authoritarian regimes, however, get by without much popular support at all – a discrepancy that should remind us of the different logics of democratic and authoritarian rule. Moreover, citizens often associate provision with the *state*, not the regime (Slater and Fenner 2011). Where benefits are understood to come from the state, distribution may do little to boost *rulers'* popularity.

Of course, even theoretically or conceptually problematic accounts can be useful if they are able to explain or predict empirical patterns of distribution. However, we find that existing theories fare quite poorly when compared to observable patterns. It is this failure that most directly motivates our search for an alternative account.

1.2 Coercive Distribution as an Alternative

Acknowledging the coercive dimensions of distribution allows us to account for distributive patterns that theories of clientelism, performance legitimacy, and selectorates struggle to explain – all while highlighting the deeper social and historical functions of the apparent quid pro quo exchanges that these models at least superficially seem to capture. Under authoritarian conditions, coercion is the rule, not the exception; it does not only begin where the spending stops.

We consider coercion to be a form of forceful compulsion in which a more powerful party credibly threatens severe sanctions against a weaker one should the latter fail to comply with terms imposed by the former. Consider coercion's multiple antonyms. It is not consent, in any meaningful sense of the term: actors being coerced are not complying out of heartfelt satisfaction. Coercion is also not contractual exchange: the weaker party cannot enter freely into coercive processes (e.g., "an offer one cannot refuse") and/or cannot exit without severe sanctions (e.g., "your money or your life"). Relatedly, coercive processes are not simply thumbs on the scale of individuals' decision-making processes. They actively constrain what actors understand as the menu of options from which they can choose.

We argue that broad distribution does critical coercive work for authoritarian regimes, especially when they are young or vulnerable. At the elite level, expropriation can displace powerful rivals, isolating them from their social bases. At the mass level, extending benefits and services renders ordinary citizens legible, enmeshes them in relationships of material dependence, and inoculates them against rivals' material inducements by establishing the central state as the indispensable purveyor of life's necessities. While provision may conceivably endear citizens to the regime or trigger shared cultural expectations about reciprocity, it does not need to do either of these to contribute to regime stability.

As Table 1 illustrates, accounts of authoritarian distribution vary along two dimensions: the extent to which they describe distribution as coercive and the extent to which they depict it as comprehensive. Existing accounts implicitly assume that these dimensions co-vary: the more comprehensive distribution is, the less coercive it must be. Thus the dominant understanding of how broad distribution might underpin authoritarianism is through a performance legitimacy logic, in which regimes provide broad public goods to engender public sympathy and support in a non-coercive fashion. By contrast, our theory of coercive distribution is unique insofar as it recognizes the ways in which distribution can be coercive and comprehensive at the same time.

We deliberately move away from the distinction between public and private goods, in part because the concept of "public goods" as non-excludable obscures the way in which even relatively pure public goods are still vulnerable to manipulation.[6] Stokes et al. note that even public goods may be *reversible*: regimes can extend public goods but then (threaten to) retract them at a later date (2013: 6). Public schools, for instance, can be relocated or shuttered. Public security can be retracted by relocating or defunding police. Moreover, even irreversible goods (such as paved roads, which regimes rarely tear up) often require upkeep: highways and bridges must be periodically repaved and repaired; redistributed land is underproductive without reliable access to water, fertilizers, seeds, tractors, or draught animals; social insurance programs must be updated to reflect and compensate for demographic changes. Reversibility and upkeep provide ample opportunities for regimes to manipulate (or threaten to manipulate) broadly distributed goods to instill obedience.

Broad distribution's coercive impact goes far beyond the fact that "public" goods can be manipulated much like "private" ones, however. Distributive policies can mitigate threats to authoritarian survival in two fundamentally coercive ways. First, they can undermine rival elites as local providers of public services, eliminating those elites' material power bases and reorienting citizens' expectations toward the regime. As a result, the *source* of distributed goods – expropriation – is often as important as who ultimately receives them. Because of their coercive foundations and streamlined decision-making procedures, authoritarian regimes are

[6] In other words, many goods usually understood as public are in fact excludable, rendering the universe of meaningfully public goods vanishingly small.

particularly well positioned to expropriate and redistribute land and other resources without the cooperation of their owners. In democratic regimes, land reform and other redistributive policies are "veto gauntlets" (Albertus 2015): threatened elites can block redistribution via aristocratic parliaments, independent judiciaries, or other democratic institutions. In authoritarian regimes, which tend to lack such institutional checks and balances, the road to redistribution is politically simpler.

Second, public service provision can bind mass populations to regimes by making the regime, and the state apparatus it controls, the center of citizens' "strategies of survival": the sets of practices and expectations that help ordinary people locate and secure the basic goods and services they need to flourish (Migdal 1988). Access to social insurance or subsidized housing, or even a few extra bags of rice, might be a perk in some economies – but in others, they can be matters of wellness and illness, shelter and exposure, solvency and insolvency, and even life and death. This is especially true where citizens lack alternative ways of fulfilling their basic needs, a situation that strategies of coercive distribution often foster.

Strategies of survival also go beyond what might be understood as the strictly material to include expectations about what is possible and what is not. The enmeshment of citizens in complex programs of agricultural support, subsidized housing, and social insurance involves the collection of tremendous amounts of data about individual citizens and households, and the penetration of state agents into everyday life. Meanwhile, re-centering strategies of survival on the state can make that state, and the regime that controls it, seem much more powerful and unitary than it may actually be (Mitchell 1991). When the state seems omnipresent and citizens expect that basic goods and services come from it and only it, a regime's threats become more credible and more ominous – and its replacement less thinkable.

This last point deserves emphasis: our approach differs from performance legitimacy models in part because we do not argue that comprehensive goods provision necessarily endears regimes to their citizens. State employees, residents in public housing, or recipients of redistributed public land may *wish* to challenge their regimes; people do, politically, bite the hands that feed them (Slater and Fenner 2011). What comprehensive distribution can coercively affect is their *ability* to do so successfully. Legibility, dependence, narrowed political horizons, and the marginalization of alternatives can forestall, hamper, and help defeat organized political opposition to authoritarian rule.

Although many types of public service provision are consistent with the concept of "coercive distribution," land redistribution programs receive particular emphasis in the pages to follow. These programs entail the coercive seizure of private property from landowners with sub-market compensation (and often none at all), followed by the redistribution of this property to the landless or land-poor. Furthermore, land redistribution programs are often broad based. Implementation frequently occurs through landholding ceilings that set thresholds for the maximum legal size of property holdings, the expropriation of land cultivated under specific forms of land tenure relations (e.g., serf-like arrangements), or the expropriation of property that fails to comply with a "social function" defined by efficient exploitation criteria that are politically determined and legally codified. Finally, many regimes that redistribute land do not grant complete property rights to beneficiaries, hobbling private credit and land markets and requiring beneficiaries to access essential inputs via state agencies.

We focus on land reform in part because it is a "hard case" for regime manipulation. Unlike state employees, who might be summarily transferred to a less desirable position, or recipients of government-provided health care, who might encounter longer wait times or drug "shortages," land recipients may seem to have received all they need from the regime at the outset. This is not the case, however; as we show, granting land opens up a wide array of new ways in which regimes can manipulate grantees.

If manipulation is such an integral part of the process we describe, what sets our coercive distribution account apart from a punishment regime account? The answer is twofold. First, coercive distribution – unlike a punishment regime – involves processes that go far beyond the exchange of benefits for political loyalty. The displacement and preemption of rival service providers and the limited political horizons shaped by turning to the state for many basic needs are defining features of coercive distribution. Punishment regime accounts tend to be silent on how regimes initially attain a monopoly over provisions necessary for downstream manipulation. Second, coercive distribution and punishment regime logics are distinct but not incompatible – a regime that has invested in a foundation of coercive distribution may, like the PRI in Mexico, then run a successful punishment regime system on that foundation. Services may be extended comprehensively, then withdrawn or threatened selectively.

To be sure, not all authoritarian distribution is coercive distribution; the other logics summarized in Table 1 accurately capture some regimes' approaches to provision. Yet existing literature on authoritarian political economy has come up short by treating distribution and coercion as alternative techniques for social control. We suggest that coercion may not be an alternative to distribution so much as an integral part of it. Our approach does not suggest that what has previously been labeled clientelistic exchange never takes place, nor that positive economic performance never earns regimes sincere support. Still, coercive distribution can reliably underpin authoritarian rule in ways that strictly electoral, quid pro quo distribution generally cannot. Cash side payments, vote buying, and other targeted ad hoc distributive methods reap few of the long-term durability benefits that enmeshment in complex distributive programs entails. And from a theoretical perspective, coercive distribution can account for a broader range of distributive outcomes than existing theories. Rather than analyzing authoritarian distribution through the usual metaphor of carrots and sticks, we find greater value in a vision of regimes metaphorically dangling worms before their subjects – but always attached to a hook.

None of this is to deny or deemphasize authoritarian regimes' ability to rely on raw physical force – the metaphorical stick – either as a last resort or as an early signal of repressive resolve. Because coercive distribution can reliably underpin authoritarian rule by enmeshing subjects in long-term programs that provide benefits, however, authoritarian regimes will often prefer this strategy to more overtly repressive tactics of control such as police surveillance, intimidation, and systematic campaigns of murder. To be sure, these other strategies may be deployed coterminously with coercive distribution to ensure regime control, especially in times of acute threat. But they always entail risk: overt repression can yield backlash in the form of protests, demonstrations, and even outright revolution. Coercive distribution, by contrast, routes citizens' survival strategies through the regime – rather than around it – and creates more individualized rather than collective relations with the state (Fu 2018). It therefore undercuts collective action in a way that overt repression typically does not.[7] Finally, distribution typically occurs through a bureaucracy rather than a military; therefore, it does not raise the specter of a coup threat from empowered armed forces. In sum, coercive distribution is not the only strategy for authoritarian consolidation, but it is arguably the most advantageous.

1.3 The Temporal Dynamics of Coercive Distribution

Coercive distribution unfolds in three distinct stages: displacement, enmeshment, and upkeep. During the displacement phase, regimes use expropriation and redistribution to weaken rival elites. Displacement is most likely to occur early in a regime's lifespan, since coercive distribution – while it may have significant authoritarian payoffs (see Albertus and Menaldo 2012) – is both costly and politically risky. Broad distributive programs often require immense investments of both state capacity and political capital, and many involve provoking powerful rivals. Regimes should only

---

[7] Of course, coercive distribution can also be costly for regimes, especially when they do not revolve around redistributing assets from political foes to subjects. Consequently, some regimes eschew coercive distribution in favor of other repressive strategies that, while risky, may be less costly in the short term.

embark upon such costly projects when they believe that they have few alternatives – a situation that is most likely to occur when regimes are new. Though all regimes understand themselves to face threats, new authoritarian regimes are especially likely to be and feel vulnerable. They may lack full control over an inherited state apparatus or confront rivals with strong social bases not yet resigned to the new order (Albertus and Menaldo 2012; Brownlee 2007). It is thus soon after authoritarian onset that distributive policies can most effectively serve incumbent regimes. Moreover, early steps may have lasting consequences. Regimes' early years can constitute critical junctures with respect to institution building, and policies introduced at founding moments tend to exhibit path-dependent consequences.[8]

Rival elites may be displaced by expropriation; but to be *re*placed, regimes need to envelop their citizens in relationships of dependence. During this second phase, *enmeshment*, regimes provide new services to citizens in ways that reorient strategies of survival around a regime-controlled state. Enmeshment renders citizens more legible (Scott 1998), decreases the amount of social control non-state actors can exercise, and expands the menu of repressive options available to a regime. While enmeshment sometimes begins with surpluses from reformed agriculture or nationalized industry, it is usually much broader in scope than displacement, encompassing wide swaths of political, economic, and social life in ways that are usually described as "corporatist" or "co-optative."

We do not contend that citizen demands for state-provided distribution or services are absent in the enmeshment phase of coercive distribution. To the contrary, there are usually some societal groups actively pushing for distribution. But much like leftist ideology serves as an accelerant for coercive distribution rather than one of its essential causal ingredients (see footnote 2), popular

---

[8] Initial decisions to embark upon expropriation, nationalization, or other displacement activities need not be explicitly inspired by an intention to create a system of coercive distribution.

demands need not be present for coercive distribution to be pursued as an optimal strategy. Furthermore, it would be a stretch to argue that citizens also demand enmeshment; hence, citizen demands are only a credible alternative hypothesis at the displacement stage of our argument. Finally, it is worth reiterating that the scope of coercive distribution's benefits is not limited to groups making demands on the state; they extend more broadly to a wide swath of the population, including the quiescent.

Even the broadest public services are not one-time grants: they require *upkeep*. Roads and other infrastructure must be maintained and updated as populations grow and means of transport evolve. Farmers need yearly access to seed, fertilizer, and harvesting equipment to make redistributed land valuable. Public health systems need to be expanded and modernized; subsidy programs must be expanded to reach new families, especially if birthrates remain high. Yet while authoritarian regimes stand to benefit from engaging in upkeep activities, many fail to do so even after an initial spurt of comprehensive distribution.

The reasons for such failures are often prosaic and intuitive: rising populations (and expectations) make maintaining distributive programs more costly; economies, industries, or commodity prices collapse; neoliberal reforms – whether locally encouraged or internationally enforced – compel retrenchment. In many of the authoritarian regimes we examine, massive distribution initiated at regime onset gave way over time to decay and retrenchment as neoliberalizing regimes proved uninterested in overhauling their distributive programs to successfully enmesh an expanding population (e.g., Egypt).

Although we do not offer a systematic account for why some regimes fare better at upkeep than others, we suggest in the Conclusion that ongoing ethnic polarization might provide rulers with a strong incentive to continue programs of coercive distribution. Counter the expectations of the vast literature on public goods provision and ethnic diversity, we suggest that under authoritarian conditions, ethnic diversity and polarization might actually increase broad distribution.

1.4 Methodological Approach

Our empirical evidence takes multiple forms and is presented according to complementary methodological logics. The quantitative analyses aim to test the observable implications of coercive distribution alongside those of other leading models of authoritarian distribution. In addition to global cross-national evidence, we exploit unusually granular data on land reform in Latin America to test more specific claims about the logic underpinning authoritarian distribution programs. In doing so, we demonstrate how our argument outperforms other existing explanations when it comes to explaining broadly distributive programs such as land reform under authoritarianism.

Unlike our quantitative analyses, our qualitative case studies are geared toward elaborating our theory as much as testing it. We present our case studies in three sections, each concerning a specific phase of coercive distribution: displacement, enmeshment, and upkeep (or decay). These case studies serve the dual theoretical purposes of illustration and assessment. First, they animate our theory as exercises in "parallel comparative history" (Skocpol and Somers 1980). Second, at several junctures they serve to assess our claims about the causal mechanisms connecting distribution to authoritarian stability. Neither of these goals requires the quasi-experimental maneuvers of research designs entailed in controlled comparisons (e.g., Slater and Ziblatt 2013), so we pause to outline our logic in some detail here.

Skocpol and Somers argue that controlled comparisons are one way, but by no means the only way, to approach case selection in a comparative-historical project. Among the other methodological logics they outline is the parallel demonstration of theory, in which case studies show how an "explicitly delineated hypothesis or theory can repeatedly demonstrate its fruitfulness – *its ability to convincingly order the evidence* – when applied to a series of relevant historical trajectories" (Skocpol and Somers 1980: 176, emphasis added). Our theory is motivated precisely by the failure of existing accounts to "convincingly order the evidence," and we aim to demonstrate coercive distribution's analytical fruitfulness as an alternative. As a result, we have not selected our cases according to Mill's methods of difference or agreement, but neither are we compelled to focus on precisely the same cases in each segment of the analysis. We follow Simmons and Smith (2017) in taking political *processes* – specifically, the three sequential processes of displacement, enmeshment, and upkeep (or decay) – as our object of analysis. Our cases are selected to demonstrate our theory's fruitfulness across a range of relevant cases from across the globe.[9] In keeping with the logic of parallel comparative history, these cases should not be taken as "tests" of our theory, especially since the theory was generated in part with these cases in mind. Instead, they are better conceived as *elaborations* of the theory: they provide crucial information about "how key concepts and variables are operationalized and how the theory works 'on the ground' to explain actual historical developments" (Skocpol and Somers 1980: 191).

However, at several junctions our qualitative analyses also serve as important *within-case* tests of our theory. Many accounts of authoritarian distribution agree that broad distribution somehow contributes to regime durability. For instance, Albertus and Menaldo (2012) demonstrate how land redistribution in Latin America underpinned survival in the authoritarian regimes that embarked on it. Blaydes (2010) argues that the Mubarak regime's distributive policies in Egypt underpinned a vast patronage system that channeled rewards and punishments in ways that enhanced regime durability. Performance legitimacy accounts would concur with our conclusion that comprehensive distribution has contributed to regime stability in Singapore. We differ from these accounts

---

[9] Our cases display truncated variation on the dependent variable. To attain full "typological representativeness" (Slater and Ziblatt 2013), we would need a negative case in which downward distribution was not pursued at all. Our qualitative evidence buttresses our new theoretical explanation for downward distribution and introduces novel mechanisms for understanding why some regimes distribute at higher levels than others and maintain those policies more impressively.

primarily on the question of *how* comprehensive distribution contributes to durability. This disagreement is not one about outcomes that can be mediated through controlled cross-case comparison; it is a disagreement about mechanisms that can only be addressed through within-case process tracing. Therefore, in several cases we undertake what Bennett and Checkel (2014: 287) call "deductive process-tracing": we look for "observable implications of hypothesized causal mechanisms [ours and others'] within a case to test whether a theory on these mechanisms explains the case."[10] In the Egyptian case, for example, we provide processual evidence to suggest that the mechanism linking distribution to durability is not what is usually called "co-optation," but instead processes of enmeshment and control that comport with our theory of coercive distribution.

2 Coercive Distribution

2.1 Phase One: Displacement

Coercive distribution usually begins with displacement: the expropriation of rival elites, whether those elites are wealthy industrialists, aristocratic landowners, or well-resourced clerics. As argued earlier, displacement is most likely soon after regime onset, when new rulers are vulnerable enough to be willing to embark upon costly, risky programs to eliminate their rivals. We argue that regimes will be most willing to bear the political and material costs of coercive distribution during their early years, when the need to eliminate rivals most often seems like an existential imperative. This implies that the swift hammer blow of elite displacement should typically happen at the outset of a new authoritarian regime.

2.1.1 The Timing of Land Reform Imposition

We begin our empirical analysis by examining the timing of land reform imposition, which serves to forcibly displace rival elites

---

[10] References for Bennett and Checkel 2014 refer to electronic book locations.

from the countryside. Not all displacement takes place through the expropriation of land. In societies that are primarily nomadic or do not rely on settled agriculture, redistribution of land is naturally less relevant. In other cases, nationalization of industry has been a more dramatic locus of expropriation and the displacement of rivals.

Land reform, however, may well be the paradigmatic form of displacement. Rival elite landowners who do not comprise the ruling coalition and are not closely allied to it can pose a host of threats to nascent authoritarian regimes. These rival landowners can fund coups, deliberately fail to deliver rural quiescence, tilt their workers to vote against the incumbent regime, and generate critical foreign exchange when export oriented. Furthermore, landed elites around the world have historically provided a blanket of basic services to rural laborers: basic education, credits and loans during lean times, access to markets, and even local policing. Consequently, vulnerable regimes have a keen interest in crushing rival out-groups composed of large landowners.

To examine this hypothesis in a broad sample requires coding discrete authoritarian regimes. There are two points to note about this coding exercise. First, regimes tend to outlast individual dictators, as in the case of Mexico under the single-party dictatorship of the PRI. Second, ongoing years of dictatorship do not necessarily represent the same authoritarian regime. Rather, a single spell of autocracy may contain several autocratic coalitions. In Honduras, for example, the post–World War II era witnessed several key changes in the identity, ideology, and policy orientation of the groups that held power under a single autocratic period.

We define an autocratic regime as a set of chronologically contiguous dictators whose rule is uninterrupted by an irregular transfer of power. By contrast, a regime ends when the incumbent in power is ousted irregularly or there is a transition to democracy. Using the Archigos dataset (Goemans et al. 2009), we therefore code the end of an authoritarian regime during years when the executive who heads the autocratic coalition is (1) ousted in a coup through the threat or use of force, (2) assassinated by an organized opponent, (3) removed in a popular revolt, (4) removed via a foreign invasion, or (5) replaced via transition to democracy. An authoritarian regime continues when the executive (1) remains in power, (2) dies from natural causes, (3) dies in an accident, (3) is assassinated by an unsupported individual (as was Somoza in 1956), (4) is toppled in an internal power struggle short of a coup and the institutional features such as a military council or junta persist, or (5) is replaced through peaceful elections.

Guided by this definition of discrete authoritarian regimes, we constructed a panel dataset of authoritarian regimes across the globe from 1900 to 2008. We code country-years as authoritarian according to Cheibub et al. (2010). These authors define a regime as authoritarian if it fails to meet one of the following criteria: (1) the chief executive and legislature are elected, (2) there is more than one political party, or (3) there is alternation in power. We use regime data from Boix, Miller, and Rosato (2013) from 1900 to 1945, who follow this coding scheme, and data from Cheibub et al. post-1945.[11]

Although authoritarian regimes are terminated relatively frequently, there is significant variation in the data. An exit is observed in 351 of the 6,721 country-year observations of authoritarian rule in the dataset (5.2 percent). The average autocratic coalition duration is 12.1 years, with a standard deviation of 15 years. Several long-lived coalitions endured 30 or more years: Mexico during the PRI regime, Saudi Arabia under the Al Saud family, Egypt from the 1952 Free Officers coup until the Arab Spring uprising, China under the Communist Party, and Cuba under Castro.

Figure 1 demonstrates that authoritarian regimes have systematically front-loaded land reform. Figure 1a graphs the number of authoritarian regimes that engage in land redistribution according to the age of the regime. Global panel data on the presence or absence of land redistribution programs from 1900 to 2008 are

---

[11] For authoritarian regime episodes that began before this year, the duration of these regime episodes is calculated since 1900.

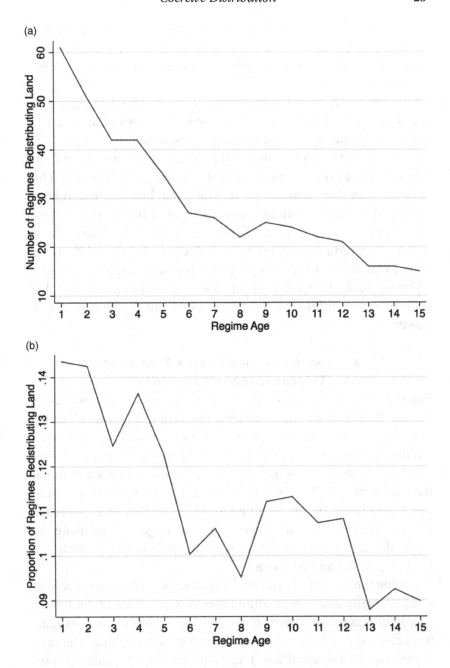

Figure 1 Land Redistribution Timing Under Authoritarianism, 1900–2008
1a Number of Regimes Redistributing Land by Regime Age
1b Proportion of Regimes Redistributing Land by Regime Age

taken from Albertus (2015). The single most common year of land redistribution is that of authoritarian regime onset. Land redistribution programs are less likely to operate later in a regime's lifespan.

Of course, the monotonic decline in land reform in Figure 1a could be a function of the fact that fewer regimes endure ten or fifteen years than two years. Many regimes do not last long enough to continue land reform. Figure 1b consequently plots the proportion of regimes that implement land reform by regime age. This nets out the fact that some regimes last longer than others. The picture remains similar: regimes in their first year are those most likely to engage in land redistribution. The percentage of regimes implementing land reform declines from slightly more than 14 percent in the first year of a regime's tenure to around 9 percent in the fifteenth year. In short, authoritarian regimes that choose to redistribute land tend to do so rapidly upon rising to power.

2.1.2   Land Reform as a Lens on Displacement: Evidence from Latin America

Figure 1 provides strong support in favor of our hypothesis regarding the timing of displacement via coercive distribution. Testing the other observable implications of various models of authoritarian distribution – such as those regarding who wins and who loses and in what manner – requires reliable proxies for which granular data are available. To emphasize our claim that coercive distribution can account for observed patterns of distribution more effectively than other existing accounts, we begin by focusing on a specific kind of authoritarian distribution in a specific location: land reform in Latin America.

During the twentieth century, Latin America was home to a wide array of highly distributive authoritarian regimes, and land reform was a cornerstone of these efforts. European colonization strongly impacted the region, heavily skewing landholding patterns (Engerman and Sokoloff 2002). The late-nineteenth-century export boom exacerbated these patterns (Coatsworth 2008). Rural populations in the region have also been substantial. While the rural sector held 21 percent of inhabitants in 2010, more than half of the population in Latin America were rural until 1960. The vast majority of rural laborers were poor, with the poorest half typically holding less than 5 percent of the land (Albertus 2015).

Between 1900 and the present, however, numerous countries in Latin America undertook enormous programs of redistributive land reform that radically shifted the distribution of property ownership. More than half of the cultivable land in Latin America has changed hands through land reform since 1930, and nearly half of this occurred through direct programs of land redistribution that seized holdings from large landowners in favor of small landholders, wage laborers, and the landless (Albertus 2015). Regimes in countries such as Bolivia, Chile, Cuba, Ecuador, El Salvador, Guatemala, Mexico, Nicaragua, and Peru systematically attacked landowners and stripped them of their property.

Consider Cuba, perhaps the most well-known example internationally, though far from unique. Upon seizing power in 1959, Castro began confiscating property from the Batista regime and opposition groups, netting 163,214 hectares (ha.) of land (Valdés Paz 1997: 81). But Castro's land reform quickly became much more broadly based. The first Agrarian Reform Law was enacted on May 17, 1959. As Álvarez (2004: 2) writes: "It proscribed latifundia (defined as estates larger than 402 hectares) and it initially distributed some land and encouraged the development of cooperatives on larger estates." "Administration cane" (sugar cane used for grinding in one's own mill) was proscribed, and the land owned by such plantations was to be expropriated. Foreign ownership of rural property was outlawed, as was land possession other than by direct owner occupancy. Finally, Article 6 authorized expropriation of any property occupied by a tenant, sharecropper, or squatter cultivating less than 67 ha., which covered more than 2 million ha. of land.[12] The 1959 law affected about 40 percent of the total land in farms (Thomas 1971: 1216).

---

[12] This provision was not initially enforced (O'Connor 1968: 171).

Castro then established the National Institute of Agrarian Reform (INRA) to manage both state-owned agricultural cooperatives and private agriculture. A minimum parcel size needed to support a peasant family of five was set as up to 27 ha., and parcels were distributed to peasants, with wage laborers, sharecroppers, and renters having first claim on the land they were working (Thomas 1971: 1216). The private plots were not divisible and could only be sold to the state or transferred by inheritance. Recipients were thereby tied to the state: private land markets were severely undermined, and beneficiaries could not alienate their property and easily pursue a livelihood outside of agriculture.

In 1960, the United States suspended its Cuban sugar quota, to which Cuba responded with Law 851 of 1960, nationalizing 1,261,587 ha. of US sugarcane holdings and distributing them among 596 sugarcane farms (Valdés Paz 1997: 81). Law 890 of 1960 expropriated 910,547 ha. of Cuban sugarcane holdings (Valdés Paz 1997: 81), distributing them among 2,533 farms (Álvarez 2004: 4). By May 1960, a total of 4.4 million ha. of land had been affected by the various reform laws.

In May 1961, Castro abolished the numerous competing rural political organizations and established the single National Association of Small Peasants (Domínguez 1978: 424), composed of farmers with fewer than 67 ha. and larger farmers loyal to the revolution. These farmers were tied closely to INRA's agricultural programs. The 630 cooperatives created were administered by INRA officials who obtained credit from the government and directed activities (Mears 1962: 12). There were 122,000 cooperative members and 46,000 other workers employed in cooperatives by May 1961 (Mears 1962: 12). The "people's farms" were mostly former large cattle ranches and rice plantations and were given INRA administrators. In August 1961, 104,000 workers were employed on these farms, being paid wages by the state, and numbers were increasing rapidly (Mears 1962: 12).

Castro followed with a second agrarian reform in October 1963, completing what he had started in 1959. This reform systematically attacked property owners with holdings between 67 ha. and 402 ha.

in size; these owners produced a large portion of the domestic food supply and cultivated nearly a quarter of Cuba's sugarcane (O'Connor 1968: 188–89). Roughly 10,000 of these farms were nationalized, constituting 1.7 million ha., or 20 percent, of Cuba's farmland (O'Connor 1968: 189–90). Expropriations after 1963 were limited to property of counterrevolutionary groups or people who left the country (Valdés Paz 1997: 136).

To be sure, land redistribution has hardly been the only form of coercive distribution in Latin America. Take the case of Peru under military rule from 1968 to 1980. The military regime under General Juan Velasco forged an interventionist, statist economic policy. It quickly expropriated foreign mining companies and privately owned Peruvian companies deemed to be in its national interests, including banks, utilities, fishing enterprises, oil, and major newspapers. The regime then created state enterprises with monopoly privileges that undercut private businesses in the export sectors of cotton, sugar, minerals, coca, and petroleum marketing (Saulniers 1988). Furthermore, it created manufacturing laws (e.g., the Industrial Community Law) that specified worker participation in profit distributions, worker shareholding, and participation in company management in all industries. The regime then set up a range of national-level worker confederations that it used to monitor and manipulate the beneficiaries of these policies.

The most significant episodes of land reform in Latin America have happened, as the logic of coercive distribution suggests, when vulnerable regimes confronted landed elite rivals. Moreover, redistributive land reform under dictatorships in Latin America does not follow patterns predicted by alternative theories of distribution. The greater incidence of comprehensive land redistribution under dictatorship contradicts a winning coalition logic. The comprehensive nature of many programs of land distribution under dictatorship conflicts with a punishment regime explanation of land reform's origins. The lack of responsiveness to selected rural pressure similarly casts doubt on co-optation and squeaky wheel logic. Finally, land redistribution has not underpinned economic growth, casting doubt on a performance legitimacy logic.

We next turn to the measurement strategy we use to operatio-
nalize and statistically test these alternative explanations for the
patterns of land reform in Latin America.

Dependent Variables: Land Reform Outcomes

The key dependent variables capture the outcomes of various
land reform policies. Data for these variables are from Albertus
(2015). The main dependent variable is Land Redistribution,
measured as the percentage of cultivable land expropriated
from private landowners for redistribution to the landless or
land-poor. We only code land reform as land redistribution if
compensation is below market value, ensuring that expropriated
landowners do not simply receive full payment for their
property that they can then invest in other landholdings. This
captures the coercive seizure of property from landowners while
also ensuring that the poor are not simply "getting what they
paid for" through taxes. In most cases of land redistribution,
land was expropriated at much less than market value or even
confiscated without reimbursement (e.g., Mexico under the PRI,
Nicaragua under the Sandinistas). For authoritarian country-
years in our sample, Land Redistribution has a mean of 1.44 percent, with a standard deviation of 5.03 percent and a maximum
of 62.84 percent, which pertains to the Sandinistas' expropriation of the Somoza holdings upon seizing power.

To ensure that our findings for land redistribution are picking up
its underlying broad-based and coercive characteristics, we also
test two other related but novel dependent variables. The first is
Land Redistribution Via Ceilings. This variable captures the percentage of cultivable land redistributed while operative landholding ceilings are in place. Land reforms that target properties for
redistribution based on whether they are "idle" or "underproductive" are not counted as redistribution (e.g., Brazil after 1964).
The same is true of reforms that single out political foes (such as
the initial expropriation of the Trujillo holdings after his assassina-
tion in the Dominican Republic). These more targeted reforms are
often conducted surgically or piecemeal, exempting some large

landowners while expropriating others. This variable has a mean of 1.04 percent with a standard deviation of 3.87 percent and a maximum of 44.72 percent for agrarian, authoritarian country-years.

The Land Redistribution Via Ceilings variable explicitly captures distribution that is broad based by definition and not targeted at specific individuals or groups. For properties that exceed the maximum size threshold, all land in excess of the ceiling is expropriated for the purposes of redistribution. Land in these cases is then typically redistributed to tenants and wage laborers who work either on or nearby properties that are expropriated.

Again the Peruvian case is illustrative. General Velasco seized power in a military coup in 1968 and quickly decreed an agrarian reform law in 1969 that aimed squarely at landed elite rivals to the regime. The agrarian reform law stipulated that all landholdings larger than 150 hectares on the coast and 15–55 hectares in the Sierra (depending on the location) were subject to expropriation without exception. Landholding limits were lowered to 50 hectares on the coast and 30 hectares in the highlands in a 1975 revision to the law. Those in violation of labor laws were subject to expropriation regardless of property size, and capital assets on expropriated landholdings, such as mills, agricultural equipment, and even animals, were also to be expropriated.

Another related dependent variable is the Titling Gap. This variable records the annual difference between the percentage of cultivable land that is redistributed and the percentage of cultivable land that is titled. It ranges from -15.44 percent (indicating a circumstance in which titling of untitled lands outpaced redistribution) to 62.84 percent, with a mean of 1.08 percent and a standard deviation of 5.20 percent. Major twentieth-century land reform programs that overhauled the allocation of property only rarely granted beneficiaries complete property rights. Instead, land reform programs tended to grant beneficiaries land with communal or collective ownership, land in usufruct with state ownership, or land to individuals with provisional titles or no titles at all. In light of the fact that secure property rights can support the efficient exploitation of land, well-functioning rural land markets, and capital accumulation (e.g., Besley and Burgess 2000; Deininger and Chamorro 2004; Feder and Feeny 1991), the authoritarian refusal to grant such property rights seems puzzling from a performance legitimacy perspective.

Simply providing one-time land grants with complete property rights can render land reform beneficiaries self-sufficient and independent from the state. This is counterproductive from the perspective of an authoritarian regime that needs to ensure political quiescence. Redistributing land without property rights, by contrast, provides an opportunity to build peasant dependencies and manipulate beneficiaries.

The most common tactic in underproviding property rights is to withhold land titles from reform beneficiaries. This complicates beneficiaries' ability to acquire private bank loans to finance agricultural inputs and capital improvement; to sell, lease, partition, or mortgage their property; and to protect against encroachment on their property from neighbors, land squatters, or enclosures by larger landowners. Consequently, beneficiaries without titles are more likely to remain fixed in the countryside.

Authoritarian regimes use the leverage over beneficiaries generated by these distortions. An authoritarian regime can create state monopolies to provide credits and agricultural inputs, facilitate orderly land transfers among loyal beneficiaries in spite of otherwise inefficient land markets, and enforce the new status quo distribution of property in the case of contestation. Furthermore, the regime can wield an ever-present threat to withdraw support from beneficiaries.

Key Independent Variable: Rival Landed Elite

The key independent variable is Rival Landed Elite. When ruling political elites are landed elites; are appointed by landed elites (e.g., if the head of state is indirectly elected by a legislature dominated by landowning interests); or are fundamentally materially supported in their ability to rule in office by landed elites through financial, logistical, repressive, or other related measures, we code Rival Landed Elite as "0." It is otherwise coded as "1." In this latter case, the ruling political elite is neither composed of nor allied with landed elites. To the contrary, ruling elites often actively avoid alliances or eschew significant material support from landed groups in these cases. Data for the Rival Landed Elite variable are from Albertus (2015). Landed elites are rivals to ruling political elites in 47 percent of authoritarian country-years in the dataset. They are rivals to political elites in 44 percent of democratic country-years.

Controls

The models include a series of other time-varying determinants of redistribution whose omission may confound the results. The log of real GDP per capita, measured in thousands of constant 2000 dollars, is included because land reform might be in greater demand in poorer states. Alternatively, higher levels of wealth may capture the infrastructural capacity of a state to implement land redistribution.

We include a control for rural pressure from below, since this may increase land reform (Thiesenhusen 1995). Governments may use land redistribution to court the lower classes as a base of regime support – especially those who clamor for access to land and pose a potential threat to the regime. This variable therefore helps tap into the squeaky wheel and co-optation hypotheses. Rural Pressure is measured by value added per dweller in the agricultural sector. The size of the agricultural sector, measured in millions of constant 1970 dollars and taken from the Oxford Latin American Economic History Database, relative to the size of the agricultural population, taken from Vanhanen (2009), taps land pressure and should be lower when the amount of land and the value of agriculture are high relative to the size of the rural labor force. We invert this measure for ease of interpretation so that higher values indicate higher land pressure and log it to normalize its distribution.

The third control is Percent Urban. Taken from the Correlates of War data, this proxies for the importance of the agrarian sector and demand for land reform (Huntington 1968). A fourth control is Foreign Aid. This may have impacted where and when governments in Latin America pursued land redistribution, and in a manner distinct from secular development trends. The most prominent expression of foreign aid came through US President John F. Kennedy's Alliance for Progress following the Cuban Revolution. This program provided aid to "attack archaic tax and land-tenure structures." It required that Latin American countries undertake land reform to be eligible for foreign aid (Thiesenhusen 1989), and then it helped finance the operation of land reform offices, studies regarding the viability and need for land reform, and loans and grants used for land improvement and rural infrastructure improvement. US aid made up the bulk of foreign aid to Latin America during this period (Lapp 2004: 32). We use data on aid transfers from the US Agency for International Development's (USAID) "Greenbook" dataset, US Overseas Loans and Grants, Obligations and Loan Authorizations. Data on aid transfers are available beginning in 1945. We code the variable Foreign Aid using both economic and military aid. Foreign Aid is calculated on a per capita basis in constant 2011 dollars.

A fifth control is Civil War, a factor that we consider as difficult to interpret theoretically as it is important to assess empirically. On the one hand, Civil War can be considered a proxy for the threat of rural insurrection that is sometimes supported by an urban alliance. As Acemoglu and Robinson (2006) argue, popular unrest may yield concessions in the form of redistribution. From this perspective, a positive relationship between Civil War and land reform could be interpreted as support for a demand-side explanation for authoritarian distribution such as a squeaky wheel explanation. On the other hand, Civil War might prompt the kind of state building that allows authoritarian regimes to distribute comprehensively, and not only to those insurgents doing the "squeaking" and threatening (Doner et al. 2005). According to this second interpretation, positive findings on Civil War would better support our coercive distribution explanation than the major alternatives.

Data on civil war are taken from the Uppsala Conflict Data Program/Peace Research Institute Oslo (Themnér and Wallensteen 2013), which picks up fine-grained gradations of conflict and in particular helps tap rural insurgency. We code this variable on an ordinal scale from 0 to 3 with "0" indicating no civil conflict, "1" for conflict short of 25 yearly battle-related deaths, "2" for more than 25 but fewer than 1,000 battle-related deaths, and "3" for 1,000 or more battle-related deaths. These data are available beginning in 1946. To the extent that our analyses yield positive results, we will need to attempt to reconcile competing interpretations of how and why civil war might encourage land reform in subsequent tests as well as our qualitative analyses that follow.

Lastly, we include Prior Land Reform, measured as the cumulative percentage of all types of land reform since 1930.[13] This variable captures the idea that the likelihood of major land redistribution may be influenced by the amount of past land distribution.

Empirical Results for Patterns of Land Reform

Table 2 reports a series of panel regression models using tobit and Ordinary Least Squares (OLS) specifications. We primarily model land reform using tobit models, which take into account the censored nature of the data. This is important given that a significant number of country-years experienced no land reform. Slightly less than half of all dictatorship-years had no land redistribution at all in this period. Yet because tobit models have some shortcomings, such as bias when using unit-level fixed effects, we also use OLS models to test the robustness of the results. We cluster standard errors by country across the models to adjust estimated errors for any arbitrary patterns of correlation within countries, such as serial correlation and correlation due to country-specific components. The majority of models restrict the analysis to country-years where more than 30 percent of the population is involved in agriculture,

---

[13] This includes the distribution of both public and private lands. See Albertus (2015).

Table 2 Coercive Land Distribution under Authoritarianism, Latin America 1946–2008

	Authoritarian Regimes						Falsification Tests	
Sample:							Democracies (Binary)	Democracies (Binary/Polity)
Dependent Variable:	Land Redistribution				Land Redist. Via Ceilings	Titling Gap	Land Redistribution	
Specification:	Tobit	Tobit	OLS	Tobit	Tobit	OLS	Tobit	Tobit
	Model 1	Model 2	Model 3	Model 4	Model 5	Model 6	Model 7	Model 8
Rival Landed Elite	11.696**	13.165***	6.097**	10.154***	11.366**	4.647**	1.453*	0.469
	(4.602)	(5.078)	(2.286)	(3.598)	(4.923)	(2.087)	(0.818)	(0.285)
Log(GDP Per Capita)	-3.626	-5.674*	-1.251	-5.435	-1.526	-3.330	-0.008	-0.136
	(2.556)	(2.987)	(3.156)	(3.350)	(2.537)	(3.021)	(0.575)	(0.194)
Rural Pressure	-0.852	0.239	0.709	0.887	0.455	0.203	1.099	-0.105
	(1.136)	(0.900)	(0.597)	(0.941)	(1.433)	(0.752)	(0.903)	(0.266)
Percent Urban	0.239*	0.363**	0.129	0.283*	-0.027	0.165*	0.030	0.026***
	(0.130)	(0.150)	(0.084)	(0.158)	(0.199)	(0.088)	(0.032)	(0.008)
Foreign Aid	-0.016	-0.070**	-0.042**	-0.025	-0.073	-0.038**	-0.015	-0.003
	(0.022)	(0.034)	(0.016)	(0.030)	(0.050)	(0.014)	(0.011)	(0.005)
Civil War	2.235	3.756***	1.837*	3.318**	3.650**	1.395	0.840	-0.294***
	(1.496)	(1.286)	(0.898)	(1.395)	(1.557)	(0.821)	(0.564)	(0.099)
Prior Land Reform	-0.021	-0.051*	-0.041	0.009	0.021	-0.043	-0.009	0.003**
	(0.022)	(0.030)	(0.024)	(0.022)	(0.033)	(0.025)	(0.008)	(0.002)

	Model 1	Model 2	Model 3	Model 4	Model 5	Model 6	Model 7	Model 8
Time Trends	NO	YES	YES	YES	YES	YES	YES	YES
Region Fixed Effects	NO	YES	NO	YES	YES	NO	YES	YES
Country Fixed Effects	NO	NO	YES	NO	NO	YES	NO	NO
Ag. Population>30% Only	YES	YES	YES	NO	YES	YES	YES	YES
Observations	395	395	395	473	395	393	419	211

* $p<0.10$, ** $p<0.05$, *** $p<0.01$ (two-tailed). Dependent variables are expressed as a percentage of cultivable land. Standard errors clustered by country in parentheses. Models 1–3 and Models 5–8 are restricted to country-years where the percentage of the population working in agriculture is more than 30%. Models 1–6 include only authoritarian regimes. Model 7 includes only democracies. Model 8 includes only democracies that have a Polity score of 7 or higher. Constants, region dummies, and time trends are not shown. Fixed effects are estimated via a within-transformation.

which captures agrarian countries where land reform is most likely to be both politically contentious and consequential.

The dependent variable in Models 1–4 is Land Redistribution. Model 1 is a pooled model that includes Rival Landed Elite and the main control variables. As hypothesized, Rival Landed Elite is positive and strongly statistically significant. When landed elites are excluded from the ruling coalition, authoritarian regimes are much more likely to attack them via land redistribution. The effect is also substantively important: land redistribution increases by slightly more than 11 percent if landowners are on the sidelines of the authoritarian ruling coalition.

The only control that enters as statistically significant in Model 1 is Percent Urban. Land redistribution does not decline with rising urbanization – at least not in countries where a large portion of the labor force is dedicated to agriculture. Foreign Aid is negative and statistically insignificant, and its magnitude is relatively small. This result is perhaps not surprising: the United States explicitly stipulated that it would not provide foreign aid for redistributive land reform. Finally, Rural Pressure is neither positive nor statistically significant, casting doubt on whether land redistribution is done to grease squeaky wheels in the countryside.

The results are similar, and somewhat stronger, in Model 2. This model includes time trends to control for common shocks and secular trends in land reform. For instance, Cold War pressures and global conditions during the 1960s and 1970s were more conducive to autocratic rule and import-substitution industrialization strategies that favored industrial elites, whereas by the 1980s and 1990s conditions had shifted toward support of democratization and economic orthodoxy that benefited landed elites as well. Model 2 also introduces region fixed effects for Central America, the Caribbean, the Andes, and the Southern Cone. The inclusion of region fixed effects controls for region-specific and time-invariant heterogeneity (e.g., geography) that may jointly influence the relationship between authoritarian regimes and landed elites at the same time as its level of land redistribution.

Several additional controls gain statistical significance in Model 2. Of particular interest is the Civil War control. This variable now enters as highly statistically significant and in the expected positive direction. Insurgencies encourage greater land reform; but as noted earlier, this is by no means straightforward to interpret. This is perhaps consistent with an extreme version of the squeaky wheel hypotheses: highly mobilized and violent groups prompt larger-scale land redistribution. Land reforms on the back of the Mexican Revolution and the Cuban Revolution clearly illustrate that demand-side pressures can heighten regime incentives to pursue a coercive distribution strategy.

Yet these findings are also consistent with our argument that civil war heightens threats and prompts the state building necessary to pursue coercive distribution in a comprehensive fashion. It is difficult to tell from Model 2, however, because it cannot tell us if these violent groups are those receiving access to land. In several cases, they certainly were not. Colombia's tepidly redistributive land reform largely avoided the most conflict-prone areas (Albertus and Kaplan 2013). And in Nicaragua in the 1980s, large-scale land redistribution to government supporters took place while fighting – and denying resources to – the Contras. Furthermore, if the Civil War variable in Model 2 is picking up a squeaky wheel dynamic, it should also help explain other forms of targeted land reform. We examine this more closely in Table 3.

Model 3 shifts to an OLS framework to examine the robustness of the previous findings to an alternative distributional assumption and the inclusion of country fixed effects. Country fixed effects account for country-specific and time-invariant heterogeneity that might influence the position of landed elites vis-à-vis the government and its amount of land redistribution. Rival Landed Elite remains statistically significant, though it declines in magnitude. The same is true for Foreign Aid and Civil War.[14]

---

[14] It is well known that under the assumptions of a left-censored data generation process, OLS parameter estimates are downward biased while tobit estimates are consistent and asymptotically normal (Amemiya 1973).

Model 4 examines the sensitivity of the results to focusing on especially agrarian countries. In particular, it expands the focus to all authoritarian regimes in this period. This model returns to a tobit specification with region fixed effects. The results remain robust. This model indicates that the other findings are not driven by the 30 percent agricultural population cutoff.

Models 5 and 6 provide perhaps the most stringent tests of whether land redistribution under dictatorship in Latin America fits the concept of coercive distribution. Model 5 shifts the dependent variable to Land Redistribution Via Landholding Ceilings. This variable captures the most broad-based land redistribution. The results are again similar to those in Model 2, providing strong support for our theory.

Model 6 shifts the dependent variable to the gap between land that is redistributed and land that is titled. Because land redistribution can outpace titling and vice versa, the Titling Gap is not left-censored at zero. Model 6 therefore returns to using OLS with country fixed effects. Rival Landed Elite is again positive and statistically significant. Authoritarian regimes that engage in redistributive land reform also tend to systematically withhold land titles, rendering them vulnerable to political manipulation.

Models 7 and 8 turn to falsification tests. These models switch the sample to focusing on democratic rather than authoritarian regimes. If coercive distribution is an authoritarian tool, then the same patterns should not be exhibited under democracy. Democracies should be restrained in their capacity to attack rival out-groups. The Model 7 findings support this notion. The coefficient on Rival Landed Elite declines by nearly 90 percent of its Model 2 magnitude when focusing on democracies, though it retains statistical significance at the 10 percent level.

Of course, the Cheibub et al. (2010) binary coding of regime type codes several Latin American regimes – particularly those in Central America – as democracies when they are ambiguously democratic or semi-democratic (see, e.g., Mainwaring et al. 2001). Model 8 therefore restricts the sample of democracies to those country-years coded as democratic not only by Cheibub et al. but also those that have a Polity IV score of 7 or higher. Rival Landed Elite again drops in magnitude and also loses statistical significance. Coercive distribution patterns do not hold under democracy.

Testing Alternative Logics to Coercive Distribution

Table 2 provides strong evidence that land redistribution in Latin America fits the patterns of coercive distribution that we anticipate theoretically. The table also indicates that the squeaky wheel logic has at best mixed success in explaining land redistribution.

Table 3 tests the alternative logics more rigorously. First, it explicitly tests the winning coalition logic using data on land redistribution. In doing so, it also sheds light on the squeaky wheel and punishment regime logics. Second, it provides another, distinct test of the squeaky wheel and co-optation logics using a different dependent variable: Land Colonization. Finally, it directly tests the performance legitimacy logic by examining the long-term implications of land redistribution for economic development.

We begin by testing the winning coalition logic. Recall that the size of the winning coalition (W) – and, in particular, the relationship of W to the total set of people who have the legal authority to choose political leaders (the selectorate, or S) – determines how broadly regimes will distribute to citizens. When W/S is small, as in authoritarian regimes and especially in narrow military or personalist regimes, distribution will be limited and will focus on providing private goods to cronies. By contrast, when W/S is large, as in electoral democracies, distribution will be much broader.

To test this proposition, we use the full set of regimes in Latin America and construct a proxy for W/S following Bueno de Mesquita

Table 3 Alternatives to Coercive Distribution

Alternative Hypotdeses:	Winning Coalition/Squeaky Wheel/ Co-optation/Punishment Regime			Squeaky Wheel/ Co-optation	Performance Legitimacy
Dependent Variable:	Land Redistribution	Land Redist. Via Ceilings	Titling Gap	Land Colonization	Economic Growth
Specification:	Tobit	Tobit	OLS	Tobit	OLS
	Model 1	Model 2	Model 3	Model 4	Model 5
Rival Landed Elite				0.474	
				(0.500)	
W/S	−6.180***	−6.972***	−2.993**		−2.736**
	(1.938)	(2.573)	(1.154)		(1.166)
Log(GDP Per Capita)	−0.188	−0.368	−2.814	−1.593***	1.071*
	(1.179)	(1.941)	(2.394)	(0.513)	(0.513)
Rural Pressure	1.925	2.657	0.191	0.572	
	(1.360)	(1.824)	(0.729)	(0.463)	
Percent Urban	0.126	−0.049	0.087*	0.127***	0.010
	(0.098)	(0.162)	(0.044)	(0.047)	(0.041)
Foreign Aid	−0.026	−0.019	−0.010*	0.003	0.010*
	(0.018)	(0.025)	(0.005)	(0.006)	(0.006)
Civil War	1.413*	1.168	−0.068	−0.155	−0.871*
	(0.832)	(0.888)	(0.393)	(0.403)	(0.484)
Prior Land Reform	−0.006	0.033	−0.036**	−0.000	
	(0.020)	(0.022)	(0.014)	(0.006)	

	Model 1	Model 2	Model 3	Model 4	Model 5
Prior Land Redistribution					0.001
					(0.010)
Time Trends	YES	YES	YES	YES	YES
Region Fixed Effects	YES	YES	NO	YES	NO
Country FixedEffects	NO	NO	YES	NO	YES
Ag. Pop.>30% Only	YES	YES	YES	YES	NO
Regimes in Sample	All	All	All	Authoritarian	All
Observations	777	777	767	389	1132

* $p<0.10$, ** $p<0.05$, *** $p<0.01$ (two-tailed). Dependent variables in Models 1–4 are expressed as a percentage of cultivable land. Standard errors clustered by country in parentheses in OLS and tobit specifications in Models 1–5. Models 1–4 are restricted to country-years where the percentage of the population working in agriculture is more than 30%. Models 1–3 and 5 include all regimes; Model 4 includes only authoritarian regimes. Given the specification of the dependent variable, all independent variables in Model 5 are lagged one period. Constants, region dummies, and time trends are not shown. Fixed effects are estimated via a within-transformation.

et al. (2003).[15] We then test this alternative, while dropping Rival Landed Elite, in a set of specifications that otherwise follows Models 2, 5, and 6 of Table 2. These models therefore continue to focus on relatively agrarian contexts where land reform is a major public policy. Regardless of whether the dependent variable is Land Redistribution (Table 3, Model 1), Land Redistribution Via Ceilings (Table 3, Model 2), or Titling Gap (Table 3, Model 3), W/S is strongly negative and statistically significant. Indeed, its magnitude is even larger for exclusively broad-based land redistribution (Model 2) than it is for all forms of land redistribution (Model 1). Across the board, these findings strongly contradict a priori expectations according to a winning coalition logic.

Models 1–3 of Table 3 shed further light on the squeaky wheel, co-optation, and punishment regime logics as well. These models indicate more comprehensive distribution under smaller winning coalitions – conditions that overwhelmingly obtain under dictatorship. This is at odds with predictions of targeted redistribution by the squeaky wheel, co-optation, and punishment regime logics. Furthermore, Rural Pressure remains statistically insignificant, and Civil War is statistically insignificant in Models 2–3.

One could argue, however, that the civil war findings thus far support the squeaky wheel logic. This would ring even more true if the highly mobilized are in fact the recipients of land redistribution. Furthermore, that civil war is not statistically significant in a sample that includes democracies may in fact underscore a quid pro quo logic to land redistribution in dictatorship. Since we cannot reject the possibility that civil war encourages land reform through demand-side logics such as squeaky wheel with our

---

[15] These authors measure S using the breadth of the selectiveness of the members of the legislature (LEGSELEC from the Polity dataset). This variable takes the values "0," "1," or "2" and is scaled to run from 0 to 1. W is constructed based on meeting threshold values of three Polity variables (XROPEN, XRCOPM, and PARCOMP) along with a regime being civilian in nature, as coded by Banks' CNTS dataset. Bueno de Mesquita et al. (2003) add one point to W for each of these criteria and then divide by four to scale the measure between 0 and 1. In circumstances of very narrowly based regimes where the measure of S takes the value of 0, we treat W/S as 0 as well, precisely because these are narrow regimes.

quantitative evidence alone, we consider the potential causal linkage further in our case studies, especially from Asia.

Model 4 provides another empirical angle from which to untangle competing logics of distribution by deploying a new land reform dependent variable: Land Colonization, or public lands distribution. The distribution of public lands may be broad based at times, but it is typically targeted: the state either creates new settlements of colonizers on public lands or doles out public lands to petitioners. These mechanisms make it easy to pick individual winners and losers. They also render land colonization subject to political forces such as rural pressure (see Albertus 2015), and even to more potentially violent activities of mobilized groups such as organized land invasions (e.g., Albertus, Brambor, and Ceneviva 2018). Land colonization under dictatorship should therefore be a relatively easy case for squeaky wheel accounts. If a threat crops up from peasant groups, the regime should just grant them public lands at the agricultural frontier.

Since land colonization does not attack existing landowners, however, it should not be driven by rivalry between a landowning elite and an authoritarian regime. Furthermore, land colonization is not necessarily coercive to beneficiaries: land colonization sometimes, though not always, goes hand in hand with new cadastral mapping that can serve as the foundation for property rights. In other cases, the state may be relatively absent from the frontier, lacking the resources to enmesh far-flung citizens in relations of dependence. Regardless of whether that happens in a given case, land colonization does not qualify as coercive distribution at the displacement stage, and only rarely does it amount to coercive distribution at the enmeshment stage, when the state has sufficient capacity to cultivate broad-based dependency in remote areas (as we will see later in Malaysia). Consequently, Land Colonization can also be used to conduct a falsification test for the coercive distribution logic on elite displacement: it should not be impacted by a rival landed elite. For authoritarian country-years, Land Colonization ranges from 0 percent to 14.97 percent, with a mean of 0.61 percent and a standard deviation of 1.35 percent.

Model 4 in Table 3 is specified similarly as Model 2 of Table 2 but uses Land Colonization as the dependent variable. Rival Landed Elite is far from statistically significant. Land colonization is typically not broad based and by its very design does not even threaten rival landowning elites outside the governing coalition. Land colonization therefore does not constitute coercive elite displacement; consequently, it should not be driven by the same supply-side political factors as land redistribution. Model 4 confirms this intuition.

At the same time, both Rural Pressure and Civil War are statistically insignificant in Model 4. Civil War even enters with a negative sign. This is yet another chink in the armor of the squeaky wheel logic. It also potentially supports our own interpretation that civil war expands distribution by prompting state building, not by signaling intense societal demand for distribution. The distribution of public lands under agrarian dictatorships should be a fairly easy way to quash potential regime threats emanating from broader society. Hence, if Civil War is capturing popular threats in a manner analogous to Rural Pressure, it should be a strong driver of land colonization; but the opposite appears to be the case. Instead, poorer countries with open frontier lands that could be used for settlement (e.g., Bolivia and the Philippines) tend to be major land colonizers. A plausible interpretation for our seemingly counterintuitive finding – that civil war encourages land redistribution but discourages land colonization – is that the kind of state building that facilitates land redistribution is more likely to occur in cases that experience civil war than in those that do not.

Model 5 of Table 3 turns to testing the remaining alternative logic to coercive distribution: performance legitimacy. A performance legitimacy hypothesis would hold that distribution should be broad based and comprehensive and structured to deliver steady growth and rising incomes. With the exception of the results for the titling gap and the lack of land redistribution under democracy, the findings in Table 2 could be mostly consistent with this logic.

Evidence suggests that land redistribution can indeed be used as a cornerstone of developmental transformation. To be sure, it served this purpose in the case of Taiwan discussed later. A host of scholars argue that high landholding inequality stunts economic development. The theoretical mechanisms are legion but can be roughly divided into two distinct sets of hypotheses. The first is that land inequality induces a political battle in which poorer agents seek to tax the wealthy and implement progressive government services that introduce economic distortions and stymie economic growth (Alesina and Rodrik 1994).

A second set of hypotheses emphasizes the economic distortions created by large landowners themselves when landholding inequality is high. Large landowners towering over small landholders and the landless will seek to avoid taxes and undermine the provision of education to maintain a workforce that fails to meet literacy requirements to vote and has few marketable skills (Baland and Robinson 2008; Galor et al. 2009). Large landowners will hinder out-migration from the countryside to suppress wages (Moore 1966). They are also likely to capture the banking system and use it to underprovide credit to small landholders and the landless in an effort to capture rents from surplus labor and to purchase land from distressed small landholders during economic shocks (Rajan and Ramcharan 2011).

By extension, much of this literature views land reform as efficiency enhancing. By reallocating assets to those who have strong incentives to use them, and by removing rural elites who commandeer the state to their own ends, land reform can pave the way for economic growth. Alesina and Rodrik (1994) suggest that a relatively egalitarian distribution of land is critical for the mobilization of savings and investment that makes economic growth possible. Land reform can enable laborers to capture a greater share of agricultural surplus and foster accumulation decisions that support growth (Besley and Burgess 2000). It can also eliminate landowners who oppose growth-enhancing investments in human capital via education (Galor et al. 2009). Finally, land reform can contribute to agricultural growth given that, all things equal, small farms are often more productive per unit area than large farms (Berry and Cline 1979; Deininger 2003).

The poster countries for the growth-enhancing effects of land reform are South Korea and Taiwan (Galor et al. 2009; Haggard and Kaufman 1995; Rodrik 1995). Time and again scholars have emphasized these countries' postwar land-to-the-tiller reforms as laying the foundation for spectacular economic growth. Similarly, redistributive land reform during Japan's Meiji Restoration and again in the postwar period catalyzed growth through investments in education and a shift toward urbanization and industrialization (Galor et al. 2009).

Yet the findings on the titling gap in Model 6 of Table 2 raise serious questions about the generalizability of the growth-enhancing effects of land reform. As the literature on property rights emphasizes, well-established and secure property rights are critical for improving the dynamics of rural land markets and achieving an efficient distribution and use of land and the complements that make it productive (Demsetz 1967; Feder and Feeny 1991).[16] Once established, secure and complete property rights lower the risk of expropriation and displacement and facilitate rural credit markets, fostering increased access to credit through the use of land as collateral as well as encouraging investment in land and improvements (De Soto 2000; Deininger, Ali, and Yomano 2008). They enhance the efficiency of land markets, thereby increasing productivity (Deininger and Chamorro 2004), and also support the accumulation of human and physical capital (Besley and Burgess 2000). By contrast, insecure property rights over land can lead to underinvestment, sluggish rural land markets, and economic distortions in the allocation of labor.

The findings in Table 2 therefore yield important insights into the lively debate over the efficiency-enhancing impact of land reform. They indicate that redistributive land reforms that reduce

---

[16] In some circumstances, well-established informal property enforcement mechanisms can have similar effects (e.g., Goldstein and Udry 2008).

landholding concentration overwhelmingly occur under authoritarian regimes – regimes that rarely have incentives to deliver complete property rights. Indeed, authoritarian regimes can more easily manipulate land beneficiaries and extend political control over the countryside if land reform recipients face tenure insecurity and become dependent on the state rather than the private sector for loans and agricultural inputs.

Model 5 shifts the dependent variable to Economic Growth to understand the effect of land redistribution on development. The empirical analysis examines economic growth at the country-year level. The model includes time trends to account for secular shifts in land reform and economic growth over time, as well as country fixed effects to control for unobserved time-invariant factors such as geography, culture, or the initial stock of land available for reform that could impact both economic growth and land reform.

We include both authoritarian and democratic country-years in the analysis for several reasons. First, land redistribution may not yield growth immediately, and regimes can change. Second, an authoritarian regime that seeks to use land redistribution for performance legitimacy may be toppled unexpectedly, yet the reform may still have its intended effects over the long term. Finally, while land redistribution occurs predominantly under authoritarian regimes, it is not their exclusive terrain. Ignoring land redistribution under democracy would give biased estimates of the effects of land redistribution on growth.

For similar reasons, we do not limit the analysis to country-years in which a sizeable portion of the labor force is dedicated to agriculture. Land reform could in part spur development in the long term by speeding urbanization. In South Korea and Taiwan, for instance, former renters who became owners through land reform could use their additional income to send their children to school, contributing to a major shift in education – and ultimately to the development of high-skilled jobs in urban centers (e.g., Tai 1974).

We measure the dependent variable of Economic Growth using the annual change in log per capita income in a country. The annual growth measure has a mean of 1.45 percent with a standard deviation of 6.07 percent. The key independent variable captures the extent of prior land reform policies that redistribute property from large landowners to small landholders or the landless. Prior Land Redistribution is measured as the cumulative sum of land redistributed since 1930 for the country-year analysis. This measure therefore taps the total stock of land moved into the reform sector. Most studies anticipate a long-term impact for the distribution of property on growth (e.g., Alesina and Rodrik 1994). The cumulative annual measure of Prior Land Redistribution has a mean of 27.76 percent and a standard deviation of 49.21 percent.

Following standard growth models, we include log per capita income to account for initial levels of development (Barro and Sala-i-Martin 1995). As the growth literature demonstrates, poor states tend to grow faster than richer ones. This implies a negative relationship between per capita income and long-term growth.[17]

Model 5 also includes the other covariates from Models 1–4 for consistency.[18] The percentage of the population that is urban taps the possibility that more urban countries could have more easily taken advantage of high-growth industrial and manufacturing activity during this period. Similarly, the effect of land reform on growth may simply capture the pace of rural-urban transformation, which when more rapid may contribute to growth through, inter alia, an increase in the manufacturing labor supply. Foreign aid could contribute to growth by supporting development initiatives or human capital formation. Civil war, by contrast, should stunt economic growth during conflict. Finally, latent rural pressure may support growth through selective investment or mechanization in the countryside. Alternatively, it could diminish growth if it deters landowners from making investments due to fear of popular unrest.

---

[17] Because human capital may speed up convergence, with higher literacy rates linked to greater economic growth, we also tested a control for illiteracy. This control was statistically insignificant and did not impact the other coefficients.

[18] A more basic growth model using only per capita income, percent urban, illiteracy, and prior land redistribution yields similar results.

Model 5 reports the findings. Given the specification of the dependent variable as the first difference in GDP per capita divided by GDP per capita in the previous period, the independent variables are lagged by one period. Consistent with previous findings, the variable for per capita income in Model 5 indicates conditional convergence. There is a positive, albeit statistically insignificant, effect of urbanization. As anticipated, foreign aid supports growth in Model 5; the same is true of rural pressure. By contrast, civil war undermines growth. Importantly, prior land redistribution has little measurable effect on economic growth in these models. A one standard deviation increase in this variable – corresponding to the redistribution of nearly half of the cultivable land in a country – translates into a roughly 0.07 percentage point annual increase in the mean of the yearly growth rate in Model 5. This miniscule effect is also far from statistically significant. In short, major land reform has barely moved the dial on growth, if it has moved it at all: this effect is approximately one-twentieth of the mean annual growth rate during this period. This is likely largely due to the lack of property rights provision over distributed land.

These findings support important previous case study analyses concluding that land redistribution in Latin America failed to catalyze significantly higher growth rates (e.g., de Janvry 1981; Thiesenhusen 1995).[19] Furthermore, they cast strong doubt on a performance legitimacy logic to land redistribution. They are, however, consistent with coercive distribution. For Latin American peasants, the political price for the land they have received has been forced dependence on the authoritarian regimes that have distributed it to them.

---

[19] Because there may be reverse causality running from economic growth to land redistribution that biases the estimated coefficients, we also conducted a series of instrumental variables estimations with the log sum of the number of prior years in which landed elites were excluded from the ruling executive coalition in the period and the percentage of uncultivable land in a country as instruments for prior land redistribution. The results were similar, while statistical tests of the over-identifying restrictions failed to reject the hypothesis that the instruments satisfy the exclusion restriction.

2.1.3 Displacement in Developmental Asia

The overwhelming lesson of Latin America's experience with land reform has been that redistributive policies have tended to arise early in authoritarian regimes, and with decisively coercive purposes: displacing rival elites and positioning the regime between the masses and the resources they need to flourish. These policies have not generally originated as a reactive approach to meeting the demands of restive popular sectors. Nor have they served to lay the groundwork for long-term economic growth and authoritarian performance legitimacy.

The region we call "developmental Asia" (Slater and Wong 2013) offers similar overarching lessons at the initial phase of elite displacement, but with some interesting twists. In this section, we focus on Taiwan, where a foundational split between the preexisting landed elite and the mainlander-dominated Kuomintang (KMT) prompted one of the world's most famous instances of comprehensive land reform. As in Latin America, this was a fundamentally coercive, not contractual, process, and it arose at the onset of a new authoritarian regime struggling to consolidate its power. In doing so, the KMT leveraged substantial state capacity, inherited from a half century of muscular Japanese rule, to rewire not just the countryside but urban politics as well, displacing local power holders rooted in institutions for neighborhood governance (Read 2012). The vigor with which the KMT deployed its inherited state capacity in both rural and urban areas was strongly motivated by recent histories of civil war and intense perceptions of both elite and mass threat. Taiwan shares this pattern with the countries in developmental Asia that we consider in our subsequent section on enmeshment – China, Malaysia, and Singapore.

All four of these cases developed substantial state capacity in the years following World War II, in direct response to various forms of intense internal conflict (Slater 2010; Vu 2010). These highly capable states have all generally pursued policies of comprehensive distribution. Yet Taiwan stands apart from these other three Asian cases in that it was spared the geopolitical disruptions and devastation of active conflict during World War II itself. Thus, its landed elite was in a far more solidified position as the Cold War began than landed elites in China, most notably. Since Taiwan is our only developmental Asian case in which a new authoritarian regime confronted a deeply entrenched landed elite – akin to the Latin American cases discussed earlier – it is the sole focus of our discussion of elite displacement in Asia.

Taiwan

Taiwan was a densely populated territory with extreme landholding inequality when the Japanese assumed imperial control in 1895. Japan ruled Taiwan until 1945 and presided over an exceptional level of state-led development for a colony. The Japanese built upon the Qing Dynasty's (1644–1911) *bao-jia* system of "ultra-local administration" to construct an oppressive yet also highly interventionist and effective colonial Leviathan in both city and countryside (Read 2012: 42).[20] It built these colonial structures with the support of existing, powerful local landed elites, however, rather than at their direct expense (Matsuzaki 2012). Whereas mainland China's landed aristocracy was badly weakened during the interwar years by decades of ungovernability and warlordism, Taiwan's entered the World War II period in a position of unchallenged ascendancy.

The uneven destruction of World War II would exacerbate this divergence in landed power. While the Chinese countryside suffered the devastating effects of a Japanese onslaught and an intensifying civil war, Taiwan remained under routinized Japanese rule and was spared any direct hit from international combat. This allowed Taiwanese landed elites to retain their strength unmolested, much like their counterparts in distant, less war-torn Latin

---

[20] "By 1903, there were 4,080 *bao* and 41,660 *jia* on the island, figures that had increased by about 50 percent as of 1942. The heads of these units were freighted with duties related to public health, road construction, taxation, and more, in addition to surveillance and registration functions" (Read 2012: 40–41).

America. When Japan suddenly surrendered in 1945, it effectively meant the end of one occupation and the beginning of another, as sovereignty was transferred to the Republic of China and the mainlander-dominated KMT party. The ruling regime changed, but the feudalistic social structure and inherited state apparatus remained fundamentally intact.

While the Chinese mainland erupted in civil war, Taiwan experienced new social conflicts under KMT rule. Ethnic tensions worsened as the KMT favored incoming mainlanders over native Taiwanese[21] in filling government vacancies left by the Japanese. These tensions finally exploded in 1947 in the infamous February 28 Incident, when thousands of Taiwanese were killed while protesting KMT and mainlander rule. Ethnic polarization was further exacerbated by the KMT's full-scale invasion of Taiwan in 1949 as it retreated, defeated, from Mainland China. Hence, as the KMT tried to consolidate its new authoritarian regime on Taiwan, it not only confronted the threat of external communist invasion but also the challenges of pacifying and governing a hostile population in which mainlanders comprised only 650,000 of the total population of 8 million (Dickson 1993: 80).

In response to this "systemic vulnerability" (Doner et al. 2005), the KMT became a consummate state-building authoritarian regime. Favorable inheritances of state infrastructure from the Japanese period would be leveraged in new efforts to expand and extend state power across national territory. Japan's version of the *bao-jia* system was replaced by a KMT-built "village-neighborhood" (*cun-li*) system of local control that served, above all else after the violent unrest of 1947, "to ferret out resistance" (Read 2012: 44). Expanded public services played a major role in these processes, "such as helping implement land reform and rent reduction, providing relief for disaster victims and the poor, and even checking on truant children" from the ramped-up public education system

---

[21] By "native" or "indigenous" Taiwanese, we mean people who moved onto Taiwan from the Ming Dynasty to 1945, not aboriginal Taiwanese (*yuan chu min*).

(ibid. 45). The provision of such comprehensive goods is best understood as a supply-driven campaign for regime consolidation and social control, not a demand-driven attempt to curry popular favor.

Much as in Latin America, a decisive elite split between an incoming authoritarian leadership and a land-rich aristocracy prompted new rulers to undercut, not embrace, rural elites. Yet unlike in most of Latin America, ethnic polarization intensified this intra-elite divide. Among the powerful central party and government bodies, the military, and the security apparatus, almost all members were mainlanders (Dickson 1993: 80. Chiang Kai-Shek handpicked the powerful Central Reform Committee (CRC); none of its members were from the indigenous Taiwanese elite.

The heart of authoritarian state building under the KMT in Taiwan would be land reform. The local population had not demanded this rural state-building campaign; nor did the KMT target benefits toward Taiwan's most contentious or powerful actors. On the contrary, it aimed first and foremost at politically eliminating the powerful indigenous Taiwanese landowning elite. A battery of new laws implemented from 1949 to 1953 mandated that landlords could not charge rent exceeding 37.5 percent of the land's total annual yield, grant public land to agricultural workers at well below market prices, and set a landholding limit on private tenanted land at only 3 hectares of paddy. Taken together, these reforms resulted in two-thirds of the island's agricultural families owning land (Tai 1974: 476).

Land reform served the purpose of regime consolidation by tightening the KMT's coercive grip on the countryside. The native Taiwanese gentry was "removed from their source of wealth and power – the land – [and] the elimination of the gentry created a political vacuum which was immediately filled by local factions, who were quickly co-opted into the KMT" (Dickson 1993: 64). Land reform also cultivated coercive dependence on the regime among newly created small landholders. These rapid-fire land reform policies were imposed from above in tandem with broader rural development policies that saturated the Taiwanese countryside with public services such as infrastructure and irrigation, electrification, and schools.

Rural state building under the KMT in the late 1940s and early 1950s set the stage for decades of robust and equitable growth, and it almost certainly contributed to the regime's performance legitimacy over time. Yet more immediately and imperatively, it addressed both the urban and rural threats that so obviously loomed. Land reform both helped the KMT "avert a rural-based uprising like the one it had just faced on the mainland" (Shiau 1984: 96) and "provided cheaper food to Taiwanese in the lower rungs of the public sector, who had been involved in an earlier rebellion against the regime" (Doner et al. 2005: 342).

It would be ahistorical to suggest that whatever performance legitimacy the KMT enjoyed was attained in anything approximating contractual fashion, or that it represented a response to expressed and mobilized political demands for economic redistribution. Land reform and the state-building efforts that facilitated comprehensive distribution policies in urban and rural areas alike were products of strategic and preemptive authoritarian initiative. As in our Latin American cases, comprehensive distribution first and foremost served the coercive purpose of displacing rural elite rivals. And as in the other developmental Asian cases to come, it turned the masses not only into recipients of authoritarian largesse but also sufferers under authoritarian coercion. Under coercive distribution, one cannot become a material beneficiary without also becoming a vulnerable dependent.

2.1.4 Displacement in the Middle East

The study of Middle Eastern authoritarian political economy is often dominated by discussions of resource wealth and rentier economies. But while the region does boast an unusual concentration of nonagricultural, oil-rich states (to which we will return), it is also home to several countries – Egypt, Iraq, and Syria, most notably – in which authoritarian rulers embarked on large-scale land reform programs after independence. In all three cases, military-linked elites rose to power in societies in which aristocratic landholding classes had long played important social, economic, and political roles. While the Arab nationalist, state-socialist programmatic commitments of these regimes are difficult to classify in left-right terms and may not always have been sincerely held, what leaders in all three cases had in common was that they faced threatening landed rivals. Here, we will follow Egypt's trajectory throughout all three stages of coercive distribution: displacement, enmeshment, and upkeep. In Iraq and Syria, war and international intervention have complicated regime trajectories, but in Egypt we are able to observe a single regime emerge, undertake early coercive distribution, falter in the upkeep phase, and then fall (at least temporarily).

Egypt

From 1919 to 1952, Egypt experienced what local political observers call a "liberal experiment": a period of semi-parliamentary rule that, while falling well short of procedural democracy, coincided with a freedom to assemble, speak, and organize that the country has never recovered. After a popular uprising in 1919, British colonial authorities allowed Egyptians to set up an elected parliament, which ruled in an awkward tripartite configuration alongside a hereditary monarch and colonial officials. Several leaders of the 1919 uprising established the Wafdist movement (after 1924, the Wafd Party), which went on to become the dominant force in interwar Egyptian politics.

The Wafd – like the various parties that split off from it during this period – was dominated by landowning families,[22] most of whom ran massive estates in Egypt's agricultural provinces while maintaining an urban presence in Cairo and Alexandria. While landowners lived large in the cities, their family estates were farmed by hundreds or thousands of *fellahīn*, or peasants, who generally had few rights, minimal income, and no legal recourse in

---

[22] As Deeb (1979) argues, the Wafd's initial base was among so-called medium landowners (holding between 50 and 200 feddans), though several extremely large landowners joined the party elite in the 1930s.

cases of abuse or maltreatment. Both the original Wafdists and the new generation of leaders who poured into the party in the 1930s hailed from aristocratic backgrounds. Some of the country's largest landholding families, including the Badrawis (from Manufia province) and the Sirag al-Dins (from Kafr al-Sheikh) were well represented among the Wafd's ranks, as were prominent businessmen – including Egypt's (reputedly) richest man, the industrialist Ahmed Abboud.

The Wafd and other parties dominated by landowners were uninterested in fundamentally reshaping the country's social structure or solving deep structural problems within the agricultural economy. Attempts at land reform legislation in 1945 and 1950 failed to garner enough votes to pass. But the colonial-monarchical-parliamentary system was doomed; riddled with veto points, the most common political outcome was paralysis. Out of these failures of successive elected governments rose a frustration that would spur and enable a group of junior army officers to overthrow the monarchy, expel the British, and shutter parliament in the summer of 1952. Though broad programs of land reform and nationalization are more commonly associated with the second military president, Gamal Abdel Nasser (who seized power from the coup group's figurehead, Mohammed Neguib, in 1954), these programs were in fact set in motion within weeks of the July 1952 coup. The new regime's focus on land reform was in no way a response to articulated popular demands. As Deborah Warriner points out,

> [n]o political party and no group of intellectuals had ever advocated land reform ... There had never been a fellahin movement ... Discontent was smouldering; but there was no groundswell of popular feeling. There was no obvious reason for a group of young officers to concentrate on this question. (Warriner 1962: 12)

Warriner notes that the coup group did have a "sincere desire" to carry out reform, stemming from a humanitarian impulse toward the peasantry. But she also zeroes in on one of the reform's most obvious effects: "to break the power of the old ruling oligarchy, with its roots in the big estates" (Warriner 1962: 13). Land reform, sequestration, and nationalization measures accompanied, enabled, and relied upon successive shifts toward consolidated authoritarian rule and the elimination of potential *ancien régime* challengers.

The first draft of the regime's land reform program limited individual land holdings to 200 feddans,[23] plus extra for dependents. Men like the Wafd's second-in-command, Fuad Sirag al-Din, stood to lose nearly everything: his holdings were estimated at more than 8,000 feddans (Gordon 1950: 201). Subsequent revisions to the law eventually lowered the ceiling for individual landholdings to just 50 feddans (Saab 1967: 17). The consequences were dramatic. Within weeks, 187,000 feddans were requisitioned from the 112 largest landholders. In November 1953, the state decided to expropriate all land belonging to another potential focal point of opposition: the former ruling family. More than 180,000 feddans reverted to the state; the meager compensation that would have gone to their owners was handed instead to the state treasury (Saab 1967: 25).[24] In short, land reform quickly cut the regime's main rivals off at the knees.

Indeed, the issue of land reform was the most immediate source of tension between the Wafd leadership and the new military government. In August 1952, shortly before the first land reform law was promulgated, the ruling Revolutionary Command Council invited the Wafd leadership to a private meeting with only two agenda items: first, the clarification of the Wafd party's position vis-à-vis land reform, and second, a detailed account of the precise acreage of land belonging to party leader Fuad Sirag al-Din (Mardini 1984: 198). The Wafd never publicly announced support

---

[23] The feddan, a longstanding Egyptian measure of agricultural space, is equal to 1.038 acres.

[24] Expropriated land was technically compensated under the 1952 law, but compensation was in state bonds that collected little interest and could not be redeemed for first 30 and then 40 years – levels that one analyst in the 1960s described as "decidedly confiscatory" (Saab 1967: 25–26).

for the land reform project except in the vaguest possible terms, and soon it was a moot point: in January 1953, all political parties in Egypt were ordered to disband in a move whose prime target, according to Mohammed Neguib himself, was the Wafd (Mardini 1984: 164). It is important to note, however, that though land reform and other legal changes had a disproportionate effect on the old political party elite, these were not "targeted" changes: the feddan caps were universal, the process of confiscation and expropriation was consistently implemented, and the committees set up to mediate disputes over land value or size were widely recognized to apply the law fairly (Saab 1967: 23). Comprehensive policies thus produced coercive effects.

The prosecution of Wafdist figures continued for years, intimately intertwined with the programs of (re)distribution that were reshaping Egypt's political and social economy. Sirag al-Din was tried in a revolutionary court and sentenced to the first of many short jail sentences for opposing the revolution. In 1961, so-called sequestration decrees froze more than $1 billion in non-land assets belonging to hundreds of prominent, wealthy Egyptians, many of whom had been involved with the Wafd and other pre-coup political parties. These new laws set a cap on yearly income, and everything in excess of that limit reverted to the state (Saab 1967: 25). The aristocratic fortunes that had bankrolled party politics during the interwar period evaporated; it was all many large families could do to hang onto a few grand properties.[25] No longer could the political class the Free Officers displaced use their money to turn the tides.

2.2 Phase Two: Enmeshment

Whereas displacement commonly involves either land reform or nationalization, enmeshment by definition encompasses a wider

---

[25] Interestingly, even these few properties would turn out to be politically consequential. Fuad Sirag al-Din's Cairo mansion became the headquarters of the refounded Wafd Party in 1978; even to this day, the Wafd operates out of a villa once owned by the Badrawis.

range of social and economic policies. Having temporarily disempowered rival elites, regimes can extend services and benefits that cement their positions as the center of citizens' strategies of survival. Health care, housing, public employment, and education are key domains in which regimes cultivate dependence, denying other social actors the ability to control or mobilize citizens. In this section, we offer case studies from Malaysia, Singapore, China, Egypt, Mexico, and Peru. These case studies include at least one case in which enmeshment did not follow from displacement in the traditional sense: in Malaysia, "New Villages" were built to enmesh peasants on newly colonized land, not land seized from rival elites. In certain geographic and economic circumstances, regimes can successfully enmesh without having to displace first – a process we discuss at the end of this section.

Throughout, we focus on the *effects* of regime policies rather than on rulers' intentions. Displacement and enmeshment may sometimes be the explicit goals of regime policy makers, but they can just as easily be unexpected consequences of policies implemented to serve other ends. As the following discussion of Mexico and Peru suggests, regimes may only belatedly realize the payoff that coercive distribution can offer them. In other regimes – as we will see in Section 3.1 on upkeep and decay in Egypt – rulers are willing to retreat from coercive distribution as they pursue other goals. We will provide some evidence of the withdrawal or manipulation of benefits in this section, but the political work being done by enmeshment is most observable in the breach, as that enmeshment decays.

2.2.1 Enmeshment in Developmental Asia: China, Malaysia, and Singapore

In much the same way that coercive distribution in Taiwan had its origins in the KMT's violent struggles against highly mobilized mass threats on both the mainland and in Taiwan itself, it would be civil war in China, insurgency in Malaysia, and racialized class conflicts in Singapore that would prompt the state building necessary to enmesh the masses on a comprehensive scale.

These state-building efforts all began from a lower baseline than in Taiwan, where 50 years of intensive Japanese colonialism had built a far stronger state apparatus to be inherited and improved. And none of them required the kind of coercive displacement of a powerful landed elite that preceded mass enmeshment in Taiwan. The upshot in all three cases would be the consolidation of authoritarian domination under ruling parties that would remain in power for more than a half century after policies of coercive and comprehensive enmeshment commenced. As in all the other cases we consider, strategies of authoritarian regime consolidation counted for more than ideology per se: whether we are looking at the leftist revolutionary Chinese Communist Party (CCP) in China or the anti-communist, counterrevolutionary PAP in Singapore and United Malays National Organization (UMNO) in Malaysia, the masses were only offered the worm of public services on the hook of authoritarian coercion.

China

Perhaps more than any other country, contemporary China has inspired the general theoretical claim that "[i]n dictatorships, as elsewhere, the squeaky wheel gets the grease" (Wallace 2014: 35). While this provides a defensible interpretation of authoritarian distribution at the upkeep stage, it cannot explain why China's CCP embarked on comprehensive distribution policies in the first place upon winning power in 1949. As in Cuba, China's civil war led to comprehensive redistribution not by channeling popular demands, but by birthing a new authoritarian regime with a keen strategic interest in supplying comprehensive public services as a means to coercive political control. As Wallace recognizes but does not emphasize in his major study of China's urban social policy after Mao, "granting benefits to the urban population encourages individuals to present themselves to the state rather than hide from it, increasing their legibility of the city to the regime" (ibid. 30). To our minds, this supply-side story provides a better explanation for the origins of policies of mass enmeshment than a demand-driven dynamic in which squeaky wheels command lubrication.

Since counterrevolutionary ruling parties in Malaysia and Singapore pursued coercive distribution as well, China's famed "iron rice bowl" of guaranteed benefits cannot be explained with reference to revolutionary ideology alone. Nevertheless, Mao's totalitarianism deeply influenced the specific institutions through which the CCP first enmeshed the Chinese masses. Two systems of top-down control underpinned coercive distribution in Maoist China: (1) the *danwei* system, in which necessities are distributed through one's work unit in a state-owned enterprise and (2) the *hukou* system of household registration, in which access to public services is contingent upon fixed and state-mandated residence in a particular district. Both systems made average Chinese citizens' eligibility for basic state services completely dependent on CCP approval. While these benefits could be brutally rescinded for citizens who proved politically unreliable, coverage (especially through the *hukou* system) could in principle be virtually comprehensive.

As in Taiwan, a critical institutional foundation for coercive distribution when the CCP captured power on the mainland was local residents' committees, or *bao-jia*. The imperative for social control under wartime conditions had prompted the KMT to shore up these organs for local administration during the 1930s, and then for the Japanese to follow suit in areas they occupied: "When the KMT regained control of major cities after Japan's surrender in 1945, it kept the *bao-jia* system in place and attempted to use it to facilitate police work, population registry, tax collection, and draft conscription" (Read 2012: 42). This would be revamped into the CCP's comprehensive system of residents' committees (RCs) after its victory over the KMT in 1949. As Read explains, control and distribution were two sides of the same coin for the newborn CCP regime:

> If the main purposes of the *bao-jia* were to facilitate household registration and to make residents themselves responsible for helping detect and deter criminals, the RCs' functions were substantially

broader. They had the job of promoting the common welfare by organizing things like sanitation and relief effort ... They were intended to communicate government policies and announcements to the neighborhood ... Their post-1949 reemergence owes to a confluence of factors: the imperatives facing the young regime as it consolidated its control over the cities, techniques of mass mobilization that the CCP developed on its own and borrowed from the Soviet Union.

(Ibid. 44)

China's grassroots RCs were not designed to be clientelist institutions doling out and denying favors in targeted fashion. Rather, they encompassed the entire urban population in comprehensive systems in which provision and coercion were two sides of the same coin. An even more extreme form of coercive distribution arose through the *danwei* system. Although only about 40 percent of China's population was ever employed in state-owned enterprises, these served as sites where both provision and control were intensified. For state-employed industrial workers, "one's material well-being, life opportunities, and political status [were] dependent on membership in a production organization, the *danwei*" (Lee 2007: 61). Most intensely through the *danwei* and most thoroughly in the highly industrialized north, there emerged what Ching Kwan Lee calls a "socialist social contract [in which] the communist regime pledged employment security, pensions, and welfare services in exchange for workers' political acquiescence" (ibid. 71).

Communist China thus developed a labor aristocracy, like so many developing economies. But the price of increased benefits was extreme enmeshment in the coercive institution of the *danwei*. Although Elizabeth Perry insists that *danwei* enmeshment did not make workers' protest impossible, she acknowledges the general scholarly consensus that "the *danwei* helped to create a quiescent, compliant populace – too dependent upon workplace handouts to undertake serious protest" (Perry 1997: 42). On the rare occasions when labor protests erupted despite this "dependency in the face of authority" (ibid.) in the Mao and early reform years, they typically emanated from quarters excluded from the most generous *danwei* entitlements due to their status as temporary, contract, or small enterprise workers. Grease kept flowing to wheels that remained silenced, not those that squeaked.

The *hukou* household registration system expanded similar controls beyond the factory. *Hukou* ensures that China's population can only enjoy the benefits of citizenship at the price of geographic mobility. In particular, the system ensures that if citizens with rural *hukou* come to the cities in search of higher wages, they can be "repatriated" to the countryside at the CCP's whim. Lacking urban *hukou*, migrant workers have typically been incorporated into a dormitory labor regime in which basic benefits including housing and health care are contingent not only on political quiescence but also economic subservience (Solinger 1999). Meanwhile in the countryside, insecure property rights over both housing and land – mirroring the "titling gap" explored in earlier sections – mean that CCP officials have absolute power both to provide essentials and to take them away. As described, these institutions are clearly coercive. But they are simultaneously distributive: through them, Chinese citizens receive goods and services without which they cannot flourish. Unlike in classic models of clientelism, virtually all citizens receive benefits while remaining permanently vulnerable to their retraction.

Malaysia and Singapore

Coercive enmeshment has been as much a feature of developmental Asia's counterrevolutionary regimes as its revolutionary ones. In the chaotic aftermath of World War II, the neighboring British colonies of Malaya and Singapore would see state-building campaigns under highly authoritarian political conditions. These paved the way for high levels of postcolonial development and public service provision in both cases. As in Taiwan, state builders' core goals were to consolidate power and cement social control against a backdrop of ethnic polarization so severe that it threatened – and in Malaya actually did – escalate to full-scale civil war. Unlike the KMT in Taiwan, however, British state builders and their local allies did not need to displace an entrenched landed elite to do so. The coercive dimension of distribution in both decolonizing and postcolonial Malaya and Singapore would be a race to enmesh the masses, not to eradicate feudal elite rivals. In this respect, these cases mirror the experience of mass enmeshment without elite displacement that we explore later in rentier states.

Neither Malaya nor Singapore experienced the kind of prewar state building that Taiwan had encountered under Japanese rule. Yet with the eruption of ethnicized urban labor unrest on both sides of the Johor Causeway after Japan's August 1945 surrender, neither British rulers nor their local collaborators in the two adjoining colonies enjoyed the luxury of keeping the Leviathan underpowered any longer (Slater 2010). The pivotal moment came in 1947, when British authorities imposed steep new income and corporate taxes on wealthy elites. These fiscal gains would be supplemented in the early 1950s with the two most extractive forced-savings systems in the British Empire: Singapore's Central Provident Fund (CPF) and Malaysia's Employees' Provident Fund (EPF).

State building amid violently unstable local conditions involved comprehensive infrastructural as well as fiscal advances. As communist insurgency worsened in Malaya, the colonial state and its local allies pressed for massive expansions of roads and electrification to aid counterinsurgency. At their most extreme, rural state building assumed the form of New Villages designed to draw ethnic Chinese squatters away from Malayan Communist Party (MCP) insurgents. Although packed with social services such as health clinics, these New Villages were practically prison camps whose coercive purpose was unmistakable. As one British leader put it, their *raison d'être* was "screwing down the population in the strongest and sternest manner" (Hack 1999: 7).

In Malaya and Singapore as in Taiwan, late-colonial state-building campaigns both extended new public services and paved the way for much greater comprehensive provision after decolonization. They were not offered as concessions to popular demands, but as proactive authoritarian agendas to reshape and control society. Tellingly, comprehensive distribution did not gather its greatest steam in either Malaysia or Singapore until ruling parties began governing in an authoritarian manner.

We begin in Malaysia, where the majority Malay population enjoys constitutionally protected ethnic supremacy. One might have expected democratic elections to yield massive redistribution from the relatively wealthy ethnic Chinese minority into Malay hands. Yet in the decade following independence in 1957, distributive efforts were relatively modest. Ironically from the perspective of leading theories, this was largely because Malaysia was relatively democratic from the late 1950s until the late 1960s. Rather than unleashing majoritarian pressures, democratic checks-and-balances protected moneyed minority interests.

As of 1969, the dominant UMNO party had done surprisingly little to leverage the fiscally effective and infrastructurally impressive state apparatus constructed under late colonialism to uplift the Malay poor. Deadly ethnic riots in May of that year would transform both Malaysia's regime and its distributive profile. Politics simultaneously became more authoritarian and more redistributive as ethnic Chinese elites lost most of their political influence and the new National Front coalition moved to preempt further popular unrest.

As in Taiwan, one of the most assertive state interventions expanded poor peasants' and tenants' access to productive land. Although the Federal Land Development Agency (FELDA) was founded in 1956, it was relatively moribund until Malaysia's authoritarian and redistributive turn. After fulfilling only 25 percent of its target number for land settlement from 1961 to 1965, FELDA improved to 69 percent of its target between 1971 and 1975 and finally met that target for good in 1976 (Kuhonta 2011: 101). Having settled more than 100,000 families, or approximately a half million people on more than 300 settlements by 1990 (Crouch 1996: 191), "FELDA stands out as the linchpin of the state's efforts to alleviate rural poverty" (Kuhonta 2011: 102). Land distribution has been complemented by school, road, and other infrastructural development in rural settlements, as well as FELDA loans and scholarships to help young, rural Malays join the burgeoning middle class. Understandably, then, scholars often describe FELDA in contractual terms, as "the economic blandishments that they offer encourage ordinary Malays to support the regime" (Pepinsky 2009: 66)

Distributive programs such as FELDA are better understood through the lens of coercive distribution than as quasi-democratic contractualism, however. FELDA has been criticized "for making peasants dependent on the state" (Kuhonta 2011: 103), but this is the program's mission, not a mistake. UMNO leaders are explicit about the discretion they wield, because it is critical to their goal of social control. FELDA "theoretically is open to all the rural poor, [but] [o]nce accepted into a FELDA scheme, settlers were expected to support UMNO. In 1983 the minister of land and regional development, Rais Yatim, lamented that 'only' 65–70 percent of FELDA settlers were UMNO members. In 1984 he said that 365 settlers had been expelled for 'opposing and speaking badly of the government'" (Crouch 1996: 41). As current prime minister Najib Razak once put it: "[S]ettlers and their families have benefited [from FELDA]. In light of this, we also hope the settlers become the backbone supporters of the government" (Kuhonta 2011: 105). Note the sequence: UMNO builds a new backbone of support by cultivating dependence in preemptive fashion, rather than by responding to bottom-up demands.

Indeed, the naked partisanship and conditionality of UMNO's rural programs make it tempting to understand them as classic instances of clientelist if not contractual exchange. "At the village level, government patronage was used blatantly to win support for UMNO," writes Harold Crouch. This included

> government-sponsored Farmers' Associations through which government aid was channeled in principle to the village as a whole or the very poor but in reality to UMNO supporters. Moreover, villagers' applications for title to land were considered by committees dominated by UMNO stalwarts, usually including the local state assembly member. Often authority to distribute assistance such as

fertilizer, seedlings, or livestock was delegated "to local *ketua kampung* (village heads) who are, more often than not, the chairmen of UMNO branches in their respective villages." (Crouch 1996, 40–41)

The upshot for Crouch is as coercive as it is distributive, since "it is often the poorest Malays who are most dependent on government patronage and therefore most reluctant to risk alienating the government party by supporting the opposition in elections" (ibid. 195). Authoritarian discretion and intimidation thus clearly color Malaysian social programs in the Malay-dominated countryside. Yet this punishment regime–like quality of rural development expenditure does not mean that comprehensive distribution cannot be the end result. "Rural development expenditures grew in real terms more than sixfold from independence to 1975," James Scott notes: "Much of it went into the provision of infrastructure and collective goods – roads, schools, clinics, piped water, electricity, mosques, prayer houses, community halls – that have touched virtually every village in the country" (Scott 1985: 55–56).

Of vital importance for our argument here, comprehensive service provision accelerated instead of abating when UMNO seized and consolidated authoritarian power. As Erik Kuhonta (2011) has detailed, Malaysia became a global model for "equitable development" during the country's first years under UMNO authoritarianism. In aggregate terms, the welfare performance of Malaysia under its pro-Malay New Economic Policy (NEP) from 1971 to 1990 was remarkable. This featured a steep decline in poverty through state intervention in all kinds of public services:

> By 1987, 88 percent of rural households in the peninsula were supplied with electricity compared to 29 percent in 1970, and 73 percent had access to piped or potable water compared to 39 percent. From 1971 to 1980 the number of rural health centers and clinics increased by 55 percent, and by 1987 63 percent of the rural population lived within five kilometers of a village clinic. (Crouch 1996, 190)

Although Malays have obviously benefited most from these policies, welfare outcomes for non-Malays have also improved substantially.

While coercive distribution in Malaysia and Taiwan has been especially evident in the countryside, the case of Singapore exemplifies how mass enmeshment can operate in bustling urban centers. Indeed, Singapore represents one of our most striking cases of comprehensive public service provision through coercive distribution. As in neighboring Malaya, immediate postwar labor and ethnic unrest prompted major new state-building initiatives, especially in the domains of direct taxation and forced savings (Slater 2010). But again as in decolonizing Malaya, these revenues were not immediately put to major distributive purposes. By the time the city-state gained self-rule in 1959, public services were "inadequate" outside the overcrowded urban core and virtually nonexistent on its teeming outskirts. The "large portion of the Asian population [that] lived scattered around the island ... had only limited supplies of running water and electricity, no sanitation facilities, poor transportation links ... not many schools and little in the way of medical facilities" (Trocki 2006: 144).

As in Taiwan under the KMT, comprehensive provision under Singapore's ruling PAP would begin with the reorganization of land: in the city-state's case, for housing rather than agriculture. This policy was initiated in 1960 with the creation of the Housing Development Board (HDB); but as in Malaysia, it only gathered serious distributive momentum after Singapore took a decisive authoritarian turn. After Singapore's tumultuous and racially charged expulsion from Malaysia in 1965, the PAP did what UMNO did in Malaysia after the race riots of 1969: dramatically expanded comprehensive provision under authoritarian auspices.

The HDB's outlays were especially impressive. Whereas Singapore's "housing shortage" had constituted "a state of crisis" as of the late 1950s, by 1977 the HDB "had built 235,000 high-rise flats and had accommodated 51 percent of the population; by 1989 an additional 600,000 flats had been built and *virtually the entire population had been housed*" (Trocki 2006: 144, emphasis added).

The purpose of this massive housing campaign was not merely a search for performance legitimacy but also social control: "Rehousing the population also provided an opportunity for the government to begin managing the people in ways never before imagined" (ibid.). Perhaps more than anywhere else on earth, Singapore's citizens find their strategies of survival determined by the state and must consider the prospects of any individual or collective resistance or disloyalty for the disruption of the services they depend upon for everyday life. Even among citizens for whom comprehensive public services do not *legitimate* the regime, those services still serve to *consolidate* the regime by raising the perceived costs of noncompliance.

A telling example comes from the HDB's Main Upgrading Program that the PAP launched in 1992, after losing an unprecedented four parliamentary seats in the 1991 election. A pioneer batch of six precincts was selected; all six were from constituencies where the PAP had won landslide victories in the 1991 elections (Loh 2013: 216). By the mid-1990s, one journalist would examine a street divided between a PAP and an opposition constituency and conclude, "On the PAP side were upgraded blocks with sparkling new finishes. Across the invisible constituency line, neighboring blocks built at the same time looked dilapidated" (George 2000: 90). Asked to justify such selective punishment of opposition areas under the universalistic HDB housing system, the prime minister was unapologetic: "When you go for elections, you must have a program. Upgrading was our program. We were saying, 'If we're in charge, this is how we want to use our fund.' So, if we lose, there'll be no upgrading" (Mauzy and Milne 2002: 94). After such tactics helped the PAP bludgeon its opponents back down to only two parliamentary seats in 1997, a government communiqué made clear that further housing development would be contingent on loyalty to the PAP: "Those who vote against good government, and yet hope to benefit from it, are free-riding on those who vote for a good government. We must give people an incentive to support good government with their votes, instead of free-riding on others" (George 2000: 90). Little wonder that opposition parties have struggled to make headway against the PAP, since there has remained considerable "reticence among the population about the personal repercussions of involvement with them" (Rodan 1996: 97).

But to what degree have fears of retribution and rescindment of benefits actually shaped Singaporeans' everyday interactions with the state? Intriguing evidence from a recent survey experiment suggests that many if not most Singaporeans continue to perceive themselves to be in a punishment regime–like relationship with the PAP, even when comprehensively provided public services including housing are at stake. Ostwald and Riambau (2017) assess perceptions of such punishments by leveraging the fact that Singaporean electoral ballots have ID numbers printed on them, making vote tracing possible even though the PAP adamantly denies doing so. They estimate that between 32 percent and 52 percent of Singaporeans believe their votes are traced, PAP denials notwithstanding. Of special import for our analysis here, Ostwald and Riambau find that perceptions of collective punishment continue to infuse voter behavior, even if votes are not traced and met with sanctions at the individual level:

> [R]oughly one in three voters (34%) believe that the ballot is not secret, but that votes are traced. Approximately half of those (18% of respondents) believe that opposition voters are sometimes punished. [Eight percent] of respondents admit to changing their vote because they fear individual reprisals from the government. Respondents that believe the government punishes individual voters for supporting the opposition are asked to provide examples of punishments. As anticipated, most of the responses indicate perceived disadvantages in acquiring public housing; in career advancement; or in school placement for their children. Approximately 25%, however, specified collective punishments like delayed upgrading of housing blocks, which indicates that even with explicit questioning some respondents conflate collective punishments for a district supporting the opposition with individual punishments from vote tracing. (Ibid. 16)

The case of Singapore thus offers an even more extreme example than Malaysia of high state capacity, both as inherited from colonial times and as improved in the face of postcolonial violence, being translated into social policy that is comprehensive yet coercive at the same time. "In aggregate," Ostwald and Riambau summarize, "the myriad dimensions on which Singaporean citizens are reliant upon the state create for some citizens the sense of a high-stakes environment in which antagonizing the state could result in substantial, albeit non-violent, consequences" (ibid. 9). While indeed not delivering physical violence, distributive policies craft coercive relationships between regime and subject nevertheless.

2.2.2 Enmeshment in Latin America: Coercive Intentionality in Mexico

Distribution need not be initially or explicitly designed to be coercive for our argument to hold. Rather, it is sufficient that governments retain coercive elements of distribution purposely for long periods of time once they realize that coercive distribution pays political dividends. The extraordinary complexities of land redistribution – which involve not only granting land but also necessary materials, titles, and continuing supplies of fertilizer and seed – provide an unusual window into authoritarian regimes' awareness and manipulation of enmeshment policies over time.

Consider the case of land redistribution in Mexico. The ultimate outcome of agrarian reform was peasant dependence on the state and stability in the countryside due to the government's coercive threat of withholding complements such as fertilizers and seeds from reform beneficiaries (Albertus et al. 2016). Yet this was not a "grand design" or a malicious long-term plan concocted expressly for this purpose since the founding of the PRI. Indeed, the origins of the *ejido* predate the PRI. The *ejido* itself, in the context of the PRI's land reform, stemmed from the model of indigenous rural communities prior to the Ley Lerdo and disentailment with an eye toward self-government, local autonomy, egalitarianism, and inalienable access to land to protect against market or other forms of dispossession (Kourí 2015). The major departure was that the state rather than local communities would now be vested with protecting these rights (Otero 1989). Despite considerable struggles over the form it would take during and after the revolution, no alternatives were seriously pursued after the early 1920s, and many peasant communities, emboldened by the revolution, demanded the formation or expansion of *ejido* holdings.

The evidence suggests that rather than designing the *ejido* as an institution to create dependence on the state, the PRI recognized that land reform would be a politically useful strategy by winning the support of the peasantry while fixing them geographically to the land, whereby the PRI party structure could visit and revisit beneficiaries in an effort to elicit their ongoing support (e.g., Albertus et al. 2016). Critically, however, the evidence also suggests that the PRI recognized and decided to maintain and even enhance certain features of the agrarian reform such as the prohibition on rentals and sales in reform communities that gave them greater leverage over land beneficiaries (see, e.g., de Janvry et al. 2014).

Several features of the reform's design and patterns of distribution make Mexican land reform an illustrative case of coercive distribution. In contrast to punishment regime and clientelism accounts, land was not simply distributed to solid PRI supporters, nor was it doled out in an individualized quid pro quo manner. Although localized demands for land spread after the revolution, accounts of land reform under Lázaro Cárdenas suggest a broad blanketing of the countryside with land distribution (e.g., Cornelius 1975; Walsh Sanderson 1984). Cárdenas also switched the reform model from distributing land as individual plots to each *ejido* member to collectively distributing land to *ejidos* as a whole (Otero 1989: 283) – a tactic that would generally be self-undermining from a clientelism perspective. Furthermore, Albertus et al. (2016: 165–66) empirically demonstrate that the PRI doled out land in Mexico in part to forestall the erosion of electoral support and to stamp out the threat of unrest in the form of rural rebellions and regionalized guerrilla activity. In short, land was not solely distributed to the PRI's most loyal supporters.

Throughout most of its tenure, the PRI took advantage of the initial land reform design to starve the *ejido* sector of the complements it needed to thrive, enabling the party to capture rural voters more easily (Albertus et. al. 2016). This is especially true after Cárdenas's tenure ended in 1940. Credit for fertilizer and other inputs for small and *ejidal* farmers was drastically cut back, while government support, especially in the form of the construction of irrigation works, went to the large commercial agrarian industrialists of the north – many of whom had been middle class and had risen up the ranks after the revolution (see, e.g., Cockcroft 1983; de Alcántara 1976; Sanderson 1986). Fear that land reform would hinder agricultural investment led to the rise of a parallel private sector protected by so-called *certificados de inafectabilidad*, which would allow landowners to seek a court injunction against expropriation for the purposes of land redistribution.[26] Land policy gradually became centralized as the state developed and the PRI consolidated. Mechanisms of legal protection became increasingly weak, and tension mounted between economic growth and keeping land reform alive (Albertus et al. 2016: 158).

This was not the *only* possible outcome of the institutional design forged in the wake of the Mexican Revolution. Indeed, some evidence suggests that the collectivized *ejido* system was initially not inferior to private cultivation (Eckstein 1968; Otero 1989). Land redistribution combined with greater support in terms of quality education in rural areas, adequate technical support, and subsidized credit might in fact have made land reform recipients less dependent politically and more independent economically than small peasant landowners in the private sector.

Yet in practice, the gap between the reform sector and private sector in Mexico grew wider over time. The PRI, driven by the need to maintain stability and mobilize peasant voters in local and national elections, leveraged the distribution of land along with

---

[26] Many of the beneficiaries of the *certificados* were tied to the PRI (Cockcroft 1983). So whereas not all land reform beneficiaries were loyalists, not all of those in the unreformed sector were opposition.

imperfect property rights and the suppression of credit and land markets to tie peasants to the regime by denying them access to independent sources of income (Albertus et al. 2016). In short, the government did not have incentives to provide strong support to land reform beneficiaries over time; to the contrary, they had incentives to withhold it.

2.2.3   Enmeshment in the Middle East: Egypt

Conventional wisdom in political science regarding distribution and authoritarian durability in Egypt has focused overwhelmingly on clientelistic patterns of distribution intended to reward regime supporters and punish opponents (e.g. Blaydes 2010; Kassem 1999; Lust 2009). For Blaydes, the Mubarak regime's distributive policies were fundamentally rooted in the electoral process. She argues that elections were a "mechanism for distributing rents and promotions ... [and] a focal point for economic redistribution to the citizenry" (Blaydes 2010: 3). In a mixture of clientelist and punishment-regime models, "[c]hannels of patronage 'filter[ed] down' from the president and reinforce[d] a system of rewards and punishments built into the hegemonic party structure" (ibid. 51). Elites competed to represent the ruling party in parliament to access rents. They convinced voters to support them – and thus the regime – by disbursing cash side payments or household essentials and promises of later access to jobs and other resources. This system, which closely approximates what Lust (2009) calls "competitive clientelism," ensured electoral support for the ruling National Democratic Party (NDP) and helped marginalize opposition candidates, who could not credibly promise to deliver services unless prepared to stay on good terms with the regime.

Blaydes's model also incorporates a performance legitimacy element. The central state remained responsible for much basic service provision (water, sewer systems, electricity, etc.)[27] and

---

[27] Residents have regularly built upon or expanded state-provided systems to serve new settlements, piggybacking in technically illegal ways on centrally controlled infrastructure.

appears to have invested more heavily in these services in those governorates (provinces) that consistently voted NDP.[28] Electoral years occasioned "budgetary manipulations ... to benefit employees, farmers, and the urban poor ... [by] provid[ing] small improvements in salaries and services to a fairly broad swath of the populace to create the impression of a gradual improvement in economic conditions for these beneficiaries" (Blaydes 2010: 77). That "impression of a gradual improvement in economic conditions" further supported the NDP's electoral performance.

All these programs eventually faltered: electoral dominance was not enough to keep the NDP in power. But to the extent that such policies did help the regime maintain electoral dominance for a time, their effectiveness was built upon prior programs with coercive effects far deeper and broader than a system of targeted and conditional patronage.

Displacement of rival elites through coercive distribution in the 1950s and 1960s had been remarkably successful. Redistributed land counted for only about 10 percent of the country's total farmland, but what had been a top-heavy distribution of land was markedly leveled. Yet with the disappearance of radical inequality in land, the rival strategies of survival offered by aristocratic landlords, who often maintained their own police forces, health facilities, and banking operations on their estates, also disappeared (Warriner 1962: 13, 31).

The state moved in to fill the breach it had itself opened. Reform beneficiaries were forced to join agricultural cooperatives, which arrogated to themselves much of the machinery that had supported aristocrats in the past. Technically, voluntary credit cooperatives extended much needed resources to peasants but also "extended state control over the[ir] surpluses and methods"

---

[28] Blaydes argues that voter support for the NDP leads to greater service provision, not that people vote for the NDP out of gratitude for prior service provision. She examines the effect of 1984 electoral results on levels of service provision between 1986 and 1996 (Blaydes 2010: 68–69).

(Bianchi 1989: 78).[29] The new state agencies worked alongside local authorities to survey land and families, assess holdings, and work out strategies of distribution and crop rotation. For millions of peasants working on cooperatives, it was state agents who controlled the distribution of seed, capital, and farm animals. As Amira al-Azhari Sonbol argues, the socialist system that claimed to reject aristocratic "feudalism" in fact perpetuated a similar system in a new form, with the state taking the place of the local feudal authority. The "feudal compact," she explains, "worked as follows: the state ruled for the good of the people, the revolution became all-encompassing, and the army had only the nation's good in mind. The government provided all services in all forms: jobs, education, health services, social institutions, entertainment, agricultural subsidies, and so on" (Sonbol 2000: 129).

Strategies of survival were being rewired toward the state in urban areas as well. Enabled by the cooperative system to extract greater surpluses from agriculture, the state poured money into newly nationalized industries and agencies. With his 1961 "socialist decrees," Nasser expanded both subsidies and price controls for basic foodstuffs and for energy, committing the state to providing essentials at suppressed prices (Posusney 1997: 70). Free primary, secondary, and university education offered the regime an opportunity to tell its version of Egyptian history to young people who graduated dreaming of a guaranteed public sector job.

In the early years, those dreams could be realized. In 1951, some 350,000 Egyptians were employed by the state; by 1970, that number had risen to 1.2 million (Ayubi 1982: 286). By 1978, the public sector and state-owned enterprises employed 3.2 million Egyptians (Ayubi 1982: 289). In 1973, the state provided 25.2 percent of total employment; that percentage continued to rise into the 1980s (Posusney 1997: 16). The resulting "socialist edifice" (Sonbol 2000: 185–86)

---

[29] Abdel Nasser's successor, Anwar al-Sadat, would later turn these credit cooperatives into "village banks" that "promote[d] the business ventures of Sadat's supporters among the rural middle class" (Bianchi 1989: 83) – a variant of distribution for a neoliberal era.

employs so many citizens that, even after years of retrenchment, paying bonuses to state employees can plausibly pass, as Blaydes (2010) argues, for an improvement in overall economic conditions.

To be sure, Egypt's programs of enmeshment were never complete. The regime was more successful in exerting its control over some sectors than others, and it never succeeded in completely subordinating all voluntary organizations to corporatist structures (Bianchi 1989: 21). Nevertheless, Migdal reminds us that the ultimate goal of rewiring strategies of survival is to train citizens to look to the state rather than other social actors as the default purveyor of the goods and services needed for a decent life. Nasser's expansion of state involvement in the economy and social provision was far more successful as an ideational project than it ever was in terms of actually rendering citizens more legible. As Posusney (1997: 16) argues, drawing on E. P. Thompson, during this period a new "moral economy" took root in Egyptian society, in which workers committed their labor to assisting the state with the project of nationalist development; in turn, the state committed to "guarantee[ing] workers a living wage through regulation of their paychecks as well as by controlling prices on basic necessities." During the 1950s, 1960s, and early 1970s, no social force other than the state – not the remnants of the parliamentary *ancien régime* nor Islamist or communist organizations – could provide the means necessary for ordinary citizens to survive. This reorientation of social and economic life around the state helped isolate potential opponents during the critical early years of the authoritarian July Regime.

2.2.4 Enmeshment without Displacement in Rentier States

Having outlined the twin processes of displacement and enmeshment, a natural question arises: *must* displacement precede enmeshment? Is it possible for a regime to enmesh its citizens without first displacing rival service providers? Resource-rich rentier economies would seem to be prime candidates for such a trajectory. Massive amounts of resource wealth flowing directly to the state might simply overwhelm anything rival elites have to offer, producing enmeshment without displacement – or, perhaps more accurately, gradual displacement *via* enmeshment, reversing the standard pattern laid out earlier).

This section considers two distinct rentier-state trajectories to further clarify the range of possible relationships between displacement and enmeshment. By comparing the paths taken by some of the small states of the Arab Gulf (primarily Qatar, Bahrain, and the United Arab Emirates),[30] on the one hand, and post-Soviet Kazakhstan, on the other, we find that enmeshment *can* take place without prior displacement. We propose two important caveats, however: first, not all displacement is distributive or even state led. The Gulf states examined here did witness significant displacement prior to the onset of oil-fueled enmeshment, but that displacement was not the result of ruling families' agentive policy decisions. Second, our theory suggests that enmeshment that builds upon displacement (as in the Gulf states) is a more stable foundation for durable authoritarian rule than enmeshment without prior displacement (as we see in Kazakhstan).

The Arab Gulf: Displacement without Redistribution

The small states of the Arab Gulf currently boast some of the world's most generous distributive programs. Citizens usually have access to free health care and education as well as guaranteed (or near-guaranteed) state employment. In some cases, they even receive land grants or direct cash payouts. The percentages of the labor force that work for the state or state-owned entities are high across the region: 92.2 percent in the Emirates, 92 percent in Kuwait, 81 percent in Qatar.[31] The vast majority of this state

---

[30] With larger populations and more extensive agricultural capacity, the remaining Gulf states, Saudi Arabia and Oman – and to some extent Iraq and Iran – have both pre- and post-oil developmental trajectories that differ from those of the small emirates that line the eastern coast of the Arabian Peninsula.

[31] The exception is Bahrain, where only 35.1 percent of the workforce is employed by the state. Figures from Andrew Leber, "Decoding the Kefala: Understanding Variation in Gulf Migrant Labor," paper presented at the Middle East Studies Association annual conference, Boston, MA (2015).

employment, and of public infrastructure development more broadly, followed the onset of commercial-scale oil production. As production ramped up in the middle third of the twentieth century, villages were electrified, highways built, universities founded, and health infrastructure expanded. Gulf states' distributive programs are usually read contractually: citizens settle for limited political participation in exchange for low (or no) taxes and sizeable material benefits (e.g., Crystal 1990; Ross 2001). We would suggest that high state employment and the way in which strategies of survival now overwhelmingly run through oil-rich state apparatuses are also working coercively, rendering citizens dependent on their rulers and preempting links to potential rivals.

Throughout recent Gulf history, merchant classes have represented a key group of rivals to British- (and then American-) supported ruling families. Though merchant classes can be internally diverse (Hightower 2013: 221) and their relationships with ruling families have differed from one place to another, in general pre-oil Gulf merchants drew their wealth from two sources: the pearling industry and lucrative trade routes connecting India, Africa, and Europe. These wealthy city dwellers typically did not hail from the clans designated ruling families by the British, but historically – not unlike landholding aristocrats in many agricultural societies – they controlled enough resources to demand a say in royal policy. Over time, however, the expansion of state services has lessened the social control once exercised by merchant classes. As Crystal explains in the Kuwaiti case:

Where merchants had once served as intermediaries, oil revenues now allowed the rulers to deal directly with the population, to implement distributive policies that bypassed preexisting alliance structures. By hiring nationals directly into the bureaucracy, the rulers deprived the merchants of a politically useful workforce. Nor were new ties likely to be forged between the merchants and other nationals because the bulk of the population benefited materially from this new state. (1990: 11)

The process Crystal describes is one of displacement *through* enmeshment: the sheer resource advantage of the state dwarfed anything merchants could offer, rendering them less socially, economically, and politically relevant than before. The ruling families of the small Gulf states did not have to embark upon the systematic programs of expropriation to displace their rivals: they simply outspent them.

While regime-led expropriation was not a feature of the pre- or early-oil Arab Gulf, it is not entirely correct to say that enmeshment began without prior displacement. As in all colonized or semicolonized environments, indirect British rule had reshaped precolonial strategies of survival, elevating some families to royal status and banning some previous economic activities, including piracy and other forms of "maritime violence" (Hightower 2013: 225). By the early twentieth century, the economies of the Arab Gulf had settled into a pattern almost entirely dependent on a single industry: pearling. And it was when the pearling industry collapsed in the 1920s, taking the merchant class' control over indebted divers and boat captains down with it, that the foundation was laid for the contemporary Gulf's comprehensive programs of enmeshment.

With no significant agricultural capacity, coastal Gulf societies had relied upon the sea as a source of wealth and sustenance for centuries. When ease of trade and aristocratic fashion combined to make pearls into luxury commodities in the nineteenth century (Hopper 2015), the Gulf became the center of the global industry: "[B]y 1900," the Gulf "produced more wealth from pearls than all other regions of the world combined" (ibid. 80–81). The entire industry ran on pyramidal structures of debt: divers and boat crews would take advances from captains against that season's expected profit; captains would borrow from merchants; merchants would borrow from larger merchants (ibid. 101). Thus it was merchants, not ruling families, through whom ordinary people's strategies of survival were likely to be routed. Rulers gained a significant proportion of their revenue by taxing the pearl trade (sometimes in exchange for protection; sometimes simply because, empowered by British backing, they could), but they were not usually directly involved in the pearling debt pyramid.

That pyramid incorporated huge proportions of society. At the turn of the twentieth century, some 22,000 of the 72,000 inhabitants of Trucial Oman (now the UAE) worked the pearl banks each year; 17,500 of Bahrain's 100,000 residents did the same (Lorimer 1915, vol. II: 1439, 243). In Qatar, a full 48 percent of the population worked in pearling (Zahlan 1989: 29). The economic and social centrality of the booming industry was overwhelming. Writing in 1904–1905, Lorimer speculated: "[w]ere the supply of pearls to fail, the trade of Kuwait would be severely crippled, while that of Bahrain might – it is estimated – be reduced to about one-fifth of its present dimensions and the ports of Trucial ʿOmān, which have no other resources, would practically cease to exist" (1915, vol. I: 2220).

In the 1920s, however, Japanese traders began exporting cheaper cultivated pearls, and the global price plummeted. The onset of the Great Depression further reduced demand for luxury goods (Zahlan 1989: 29). Coastal economies were thrown into chaos; both merchants and rulers – to say nothing of ordinary pearl divers and their families – were suddenly short on cash. Pyramids of debt began to crumble and rulers, deprived of their tax revenues, could do little to stop the process (Hightower 2013: 224).

Apart from Kuwait, where merchants had a firmer foundation in non-pearling trade,[32] the Gulf societies were severely disrupted. Qatar, in particular, seemed to be disappearing: without pearling to anchor the economy, "the population fell dramatically, from 27,000 at the beginning of the [twentieth] century to 16,000, possibly lower, by 1949" (Crystal 1990: 117). Emigration removed the last vestige of a local trading community" (ibid. 117), leaving the capital, Doha, "little more than a miserable fishing village . . . more than half in ruins," according to the British Political Resident (Hay 1955: 110, quoted in Crystal 1990: 117). Whatever control structures of indebtedness had granted merchants over pearling workers began

---

[32] Our thanks to Sean Yom for drawing our attention to this point.

to evaporate. "When the merchants lost the pearl divers," Crystal writes, "they lost their autonomous political clout, and they lost the ability to threaten to leave, taking with them a sizable portion of the population" (ibid. 11).

It was against this backdrop that oil concessions began to be signed in the 1930s. Advances on concessions came just in time to rescue floundering economies: the Gulf's *deus ex machina*, in Zahlan's words (1989: 49). When oil came to the Gulf, therefore, it did not come into thriving economies with long-standing strategies of survival intact. It came into societies in which dominant modes and techniques of social control had begun to falter – if not collapse entirely. Without either resources or social control that could rival even embryonic welfare states, merchants were easily outmaneuvered (though not, to be sure, permanently silenced). The massive resource advantage granted by oil and natural gas has certainly allowed Arab Gulf regimes to reorient citizens' strategies of survival through the state. But in the UAE, Qatar, and Bahrain, the work of displacement was well underway before enmeshment began.

The importance of pre-oil displacement is underscored by the one state in which it did not truly take place: Kuwait, where merchants had a firmer financial footing and were not wiped out by the pearling crash. There, it took particularly massive outlays of (oil-fueled) state resources to reroute strategies of survival through the state. A program of land reform in the 1950s granted the state title to land it would need to build public infrastructure – but rulers paid handsomely for the land they took, leaving many wealthy merchants even richer (Crystal 1990: 8, 76–77). While Kuwait's merchant classes cannot rival the distributive capacity of a full-blown rentier welfare state, the country's politics has been permanently marked by the fact that they were never truly displaced (see Yom 2015: ch. 3).

Kazakhstan: Enmeshment without Displacement

Not all resource-rich economies experienced the kind of disruption that preceded the discovery of oil in the Gulf. To consider what oil-fueled enmeshment without displacement looks like, however, we must travel farther afield, to post-Soviet Central Asia. In Kazakhstan,[33] resource wealth was layered on top of existing patterns of social control and organization, reinforcing rather than displacing potential rivals. While President Nursultan Nazarbayev's system has held thus far, our theory suggests that the Kazakhstani regime – which never thoroughly displaced its rivals – will be more vulnerable than the Gulf states described earlier to fluctuations in oil revenues. In much of the Gulf, rival service providers have essentially been eliminated; in Kazakhstan, they remain relevant to citizens' ability to survive.

For centuries, clans – kinship-based groups of varying sizes – have served as major loci of social organization across Central Asia. Soviet-era policies in what is now Kazakhstan aimed to disrupt systems of kinship organization (Burn 2006: 112) and certainly deprived clans of much of their public political and social weight (Schatz 2004: 96–97). Nevertheless, the constant shortages caused by state socialism provided a new way for clans to support their members. Clans began to serve as networks competing to secure access to limited goods. "Soviet-era shortages," Schatz writes, "edged kinship into certain niches; it now served to provide access to goods (political power, inputs for industry, consumer products, for example) that were in potentially short supply" (ibid. 239). What looked like Soviet-style reorganization was in fact a continuation of clan relevance: "many clan leaders became the administrators of collective farms or factories," and "[c]lan members formed the workforce under their previous community leaders, cast in new roles, refining the[ir] strategies of action to function with the Soviet structure, strengthening the cohesion of the groups" (Burn 2006: 114). Clans even gained an edge over other kinds of social organization precisely because clan identity in Kazakhstan was not ascriptive: "[c]lan background could thus be *concealed* from the agents of Soviet surveillance who prosecuted network behavior as illegal" (Schatz 2004: 17).

---

[33] We thank Zahabya Mama for bringing the relevance of the Kazakhstani case to our attention.

When the Soviet Union collapsed and Kazakhstan became independent in 1991, "clans and factions were still controlling resource networks and facilitating social exchange in all parts of Central Asia" (Burn 2006: 118). In the Gulf, many rival service providers were already struggling before oil revenues arrived; in Kazakhstan, clans had managed to remain relevant throughout the Soviet era and showed no sign of weakening. Independent Kazakhstan came into being with meager oil resources, but over the course of the next decade new fields were discovered and global prices rose: Kazakhstan now ranks twelfth in the world in terms of proven reserves (United States Energy Information Administration 2017: 3). As in the Gulf, state-based provision programs were quick to follow. Social service spending more than quintupled, rising from $4 billion a year in 1999 to $25 billion in 2007 (Palazuelos and Fernandez 2012: 30).

Nevertheless, even the newly wealthy Kazakhstani state could not do what the newly rich royal families of the Gulf could: "bypass traditional alliance structures" (Crystal 1990: 11). Rather than displacing clan elites, Nazarbayev's state absorbed them. While the president evinced a preference for his own extended family, and frequently rotated provincial governors, "he also sought to avoid a fundamental imbalance in the relative power of the three umbrella clans" – effectively preserving their relevance rather than displacing them (Schatz 2004: 104, 95). In such a situation, contractual theories of authoritarianism do have some traction: what Nazarbaev has done is to incorporate existing providers of social services into the state apparatus by offering them resources. "Kin background," Burn observes, "[became] a primary consideration in political patronage"; clan elites were appointed to state positions and then worked to hire their own clanspeople (2006: 107). Under continuing conditions of authoritarian uncertainty, "clans serve as an alternative to formal market institutions and official bureaucracies" for citizens looking to find employment, secure access to resources, and otherwise survive in contemporary Kazakhstan (Collins 2002: 142).

To be sure, Kazakhstan's history as a major oil exporter dates only to the 1990s; the Gulf states, which began exporting oil as early as the 1930s, have had significantly more time to wear away rivals through overwhelming service provision. Yet so long as clans remain useful to citizens trying to access *state* resources, it seems unlikely that they will lose their relevance. Insofar as we have argued throughout that coercive distribution is a more stable foundation for authoritarian rule than simple payoffs, there is reason to believe that Kazakhstan's rentier state is more precariously positioned than its Gulf counterparts.

3 Phase Three: Upkeep

In this final empirical section, we trace the effect of decaying coercive distribution policies on authoritarian regime durability. Although it is beyond our reach to offer a systematic theory for why some regimes perform better than others at upkeep, the following discussion of Egypt should illustrate how coercive distribution contributes to regime durability, and how its decay can signal trouble for regime survival.

3.1 Egypt: Neoliberal Decay and Popular Uprising

The Egyptian regime's retreat from its ambitious distributive programs began soon after Gamal Abdel Nasser's death in 1970. President Anwar al-Sadat's neoliberal "opening" policies and pivot toward the anti-communist West initiated the process of state retreat in the 1970s. The fall of the Soviet Union and a heavily conditioned 1991 International Monetary Fund (IMF) loan furthered ongoing processes of disengaging the state from its social service activities. Meanwhile, the Egyptian population (and, given the country's unique geography, its effective population density) increased in ways that would strain the capacities of any state apparatus. Egypt's population has nearly tripled since 1970; while Mitchell (2002: 213–15) rightly notes that subsequent distribution problems were in part the result of overconsumption by the wealthy, it is nevertheless true that more births strained existing hospital and school facilities.

The purported promise of state employment upon graduation from university remains an aspiration for many young people, despite the fact that salaries are low and benefits stingy. For all but a handful of graduates every year, that dream is now an impossible one; even the lucky often wait years for an entry-level appointment. Subsidy programs were frozen in the last years of the Mubarak regime; while existing families could still access cut-rate sugar and oil, for example, newlyweds were left to fend for themselves in the market. Public funding and other forms of indirect support for syndicates began to falter, putting at risk the benefits – pensions, cheap housing, even budget vacations – that those syndicates traditionally provided to their members.[34]

In the wake of this massive (albeit uneven) retrenchment of the state, spaces of increased autonomy grew throughout Egyptian society. In these spaces, citizens built strategies of survival that either excluded the state or afforded it a much smaller role. Moreover, state retrenchment did not necessarily mean that citizens turned to the market to fulfill their basic needs. In the 1980s and 1990s, farmers exposed to agricultural deregulation moved "not toward the market but toward increased self-provisioning and protection from the market" (Mitchell 1998: 23). These peasant families turned not to cash crops but to subsistence staples, especially wheat, rice, and alfalfa for cattle (ibid. 23). Insulated from price manipulations and insured against retaliation by subsistence agriculture, such farmers become ever so slightly harder for the regime to threaten.

Similar processes have taken place in cities. As the population exploded but remained confined to the narrow strips of habitable land along the Nile, citizens built illegal settlements on agricultural land rather than waiting for scarce and impractical public housing. The residents of what are now called "haphazard" or "popular"

---

[34] Indeed, a number of syndicates are currently on the brink of bankruptcy. See Aya Daabas, "*Al-iflas yutarid al-niqabat al-mihaniyya . . . wal-hukuma: la haya li-man yunadi*" *Sawt al-Umma*, March 31, 2017.

quarters often tapped into city infrastructure or expanded it to serve their new homes, siphoning off water and electricity from the central grid. These popular quarters have long been painted in Egyptian media and international development discourse as spaces of violence, havoc, and social ills (see Sims 2010), but more recent work by scholars familiar with everyday life in these neighborhoods has suggested that they are in fact places of considerable order – an order that does not come via state imposition and organization but instead from the creation of autonomous strategies of survival. Social policing keeps street harassment lower than in downtown Cairo; informally appointed mediators try to solve interfamily conflicts without involving the police, and community lending circles help young people pay for marriage expenses. None of these strategies is without its own flaws, but taken together they represent a system that combines "community-based institutions and mechanisms of dispute management, the local enforcement of social norms of interaction and social support networks" (Ismail 2013: 871). The state is no longer relied upon to play this key social role.

It is in such popular neighborhoods that Islamist groups, in particular, have had considerable success parlaying social service provision into political support. In the 1990s, the Gama'a Islamiyya had so thoroughly reoriented strategies of survival in one part of the informal neighborhood of Imbaba that they announced to the international press the formation of the "Islamic Republic of Imbaba" (the state responded with a massive police siege, its overwhelming monopoly on force intact).

Young people in the popular quarters – some hardened soccer hooligans, others simply informally employed and tired of being harassed by police – played a critical role in supporting Egypt's January 2011 uprising. Though the protests in Cairo's central squares and their photogenic "middle-class" activists captured a great deal of attention, protesters were only able to hold Tahrir because the police had been "defeated" by battles in informal areas (el-Ghobashy 2011). "[I]n the back streets of Tahrir and the popular quarters," Ismail writes, "assaults on police stations took place primarily in densely populated areas long stigmatized in official public discourse for being part of the city's *"ashwa'iyyat'* (literally 'haphazard communities') such as Bulaq al-Dakrur, Matariyya, and Imbaba ... These attacks aimed to both settle accounts with the police and disarm them so that the protests could continue" (Ismail 2013: 872). Neither the blunt coercion of the police nor the presence of clientelist chains of exchange could prevent more autonomous popular quarters from erupting into active opposition.

Meanwhile, non-state strategies of survival were activated all over Cairo. The Mubarak regime's primary response to the 2011 uprising was to retract the state's provision of a key public good – security – and to assume that citizens in precarious economic circumstances would not tolerate paralysis or disruption for long. Yet many Egyptians had been learning to live without the state for years, if not decades. Subsistence crops and household farming meant that many families were slightly less dependent on the paralyzed cash economy for food. The Muslim Brotherhood sprang into action not only in Tahrir Square but also in the neighborhoods, providing supplies for families that might otherwise have turned against the disruptive protests.[35] Just as protesters holding major squares organized to provide security, so too did neighborhoods, where "popular committees" sprang up, setting up roadblocks, directing traffic, and deterring looting and other crime. Regime threats to withhold state-provided goods lose much of their force when those goods – whether security, food, or employment – are available elsewhere. That the Egyptian regime's failure to maintain control stemmed in part from citizens' resort to autonomous strategies of survival serves to emphasize the coercive value of what might superficially look like contractual material exchange.

There is one branch of the Egyptian state, however, that has never abandoned its commitment to providing comprehensive strategies of survival to the citizens in its ambit – and, not coincidentally, it is the branch that currently reigns supreme. Though

---

[35] Interview (Sofia Fenner), MB member, Agouza, summer 2012.

much ink has been spilled on the Egyptian military's economic "empire" of businesses, factories, and other profit-generating operations, the fact that the military also offers a comprehensive set of benefits to its officer corps (conscripts are not so lucky) is often overlooked. Special schools, hospitals – among Egypt's best – and even hotels and wedding venues are available only to military officers and their families. Thus far, the military has not embarked upon a major project of enmeshment vis-à-vis the civilian population, but there are signs that it is, at least, engaging in displacement. Military-made products, which can be sold at low prices because they are produced by unpaid conscript labor, help keep basic goods accessible to ordinary citizens even as the civilian government of former general Abdel Fattah al-Sisi lifts subsidies and floats the currency. To be sure, selling military-made pasta does not provide nearly the same legibility benefits as enmeshing a worker in a public sector job; even Nasser's attempts at enmeshment had greater stability benefits than the military's indirect practices of displacement. What keeps rival service providers from emerging for the moment, at least, is raw repression.

4 Conclusion

Contrary to leading theories in political economy, authoritarian regimes frequently distribute resources to the many rather than hoarding them among the few. And contrary to the current wave of literature that aims to explain why authoritarian regimes often do distribute economic resources to the poor, these regimes do not pursue such distribution through the same contractual logic or with the same liberating or legitimating consequences as democracies.

We have argued that coercive distribution – in all three of its stages – powerfully underpins durable authoritarian rule. What we have not done is offer a systematic causal account for variation in coercive distribution across space and time, beyond our claim that coalitional splits between ruling and landed elites best explain the onset of coercive displacement policies in the countryside, and that state capacity underpins the effective enmeshment of the masses in regime-spun webs of distribution. Offering such an account must surely be the natural next step for research on authoritarian distribution. Given its many authoritarian advantages, why have some regimes embarked upon programs of coercive distribution while others have not? Why are some enmeshment policies more comprehensive or generous than others? And why have regimes been variably successful at maintaining coercive distribution policies over time?

The most effective way to tackle these questions would be to examine negative cases at each of the three stages, taking into account cases in which displacement was never seriously attempted (e.g., Pakistan under various military regimes), cases in which displacement occurred but significant enmeshment never followed (e.g., Libya), and those in which initial attempts at coercive distribution were not matched by a political commitment to upkeep and maintenance (here, Egypt is a prime example among our cases). Such research would also need to expand its empirical focus to carefully examine regime decision-making processes – a methodologically challenging task when the regimes in question are authoritarian – and the vicissitudes of policy implementation. While such an undertaking is beyond our scope here, the empirical evidence we do have suggests several preliminary answers to these causal questions.

As far as onset is concerned, we draw on Albertus (2015) and our analysis here to argue that elite splits are a leading cause of initial programs of displacement. We have shown with both quantitative and qualitative evidence that coalitional splits between ruling elites and aristocratic, landholding rivals are a key trigger for extensive programs of land redistribution; we suspect the same should hold true with other forms of elite displacement as well. In some of our cases, additionally, leftist ideology seems to play a contributory role in facilitating the introduction and implementation of land reform and other redistributive programs. The availability – and popularity – of an ideological justification for the seizure of rival elite assets no doubt contributed to the thoroughness of displacement in communist Cuba and China, for example. Even in cases of more ambiguous programmatic commitments – such as Abdel Nasser's uneasy fusion of Islamism, socialism, and Arab nationalism – land reform was painted not (just) as an attack on rivals but also as consistent with the young regime's overall orientation. That said, and again as Albertus observes in Latin America, leftist ideology is by no means a necessary condition for displacement: many right-wing regimes have jumped at the chance to expropriate their elite rivals as well.

Explaining variation in the extent of enmeshment is a trickier proposition. The extent to which regimes are able to entrap their citizens in relationships of dependence depends not only on political will but also on the state's infrastructural capacity, economic abundance, population growth, and even geography. Enmeshment is a process likely to exhibit a great deal of equifinality in both its extent and generosity. The more encompassing programs we have discussed – Malaysia's and Singapore's, for example – seem to have been motivated by particularly threatening and persistent ethnic tensions that at times escalated to outright civil war. But when we turned our attentions to rentier states such as Kuwait or Qatar, we found that some regimes offer generous enmeshment programs because the resources to do so are readily available (and considered part of national patrimony).

In general, however, our cases suggest a recursive relationship between state capacity and the extent of enmeshment. Whether due to colonial inheritance, the pressures of internal or external warfare, or other more contingent factors, some postcolonial authoritarian regimes came to power with much stronger state apparatuses than others. These infrastructural Leviathans provide ideal vehicles for authoritarian rulers to establish and maintain coercive control over the masses through monopolistic control over circuits of downward economic distribution. Where authoritarian regimes were initially backed by strong states, they are more able to cultivate lasting dependency among their citizens. In turn, every expansion of enmeshment renders the state apparatus not only larger but also more central to their subjects' survival strategies. Enmeshment is thus one of a number of ways in which strong states – and the authoritarian regimes that run them – tend to get stronger over time.

It is on the question of why regimes display different levels of commitment to upkeep where we are most cautious about drawing strong causal conclusions. Why have rulers in Singapore continued to invest in and update their coercive distribution programs, while regimes such as Egypt's have abandoned such maintenance – and paid a high price in terms of regime stability? There can obviously be no monocausal explanation for a phenomenon as complex as the political commitment to high levels of authoritarian distribution. Our cases suggest, however, that sustained upkeep is probably the exception. Internationally mandated structural adjustment and austerity programs, global trends toward welfare state retrenchment, and growing populations have posed insurmountable challenges to upkeep in a range of countries – Egypt being our prime example. Yet in some cases, such as those from developmental Asia, regimes have prioritized upkeep despite fiscal challenges.

We suggest that these unusual levels of commitment to upkeep might have at least one surprising source: ethnic polarization. Whereas democracies are widely theorized to cater to electoral majorities (and therefore fail to distribute to electorally irrelevant minority groups), authoritarian regimes must remain vigilant to threats of both elite challenge and mass upheaval. Ethnic polarization tends both to exacerbate these threats and to remain a feature of social life over time (Slater 2010). While aggressive programs of displacement might sideline a merchant or aristocratic class once and for all, such programs will usually not erase ethnic diversity or polarization. Even when the predominant model of distribution is ethnocracy rather than coercive distribution – insofar as public spending is overwhelmingly targeted to a favored ethnic majority over a "second class" ethnic minority – enduring ethnic rivalries might make generous provision to the ruling majority a stronger ongoing imperative.[36]

---

[36] Among cases considered here, Malaysia is the best example of coercive distribution decaying into ethnocracy over time, yet still maintaining relatively

This casts the difference between authoritarian and democratic distribution in particularly sharp relief. Under conditions of ethnic polarization, authoritarian regimes have more (not less) incentive to ensure that coercive distribution is not allowed to decay or break down over time. Indeed – and this presents an important avenue for further research – ethnic polarization may even provide rulers with the incentive to make initial displacement more thorough-going and subsequent enmeshment more encompassing. When assessing our central argument that authoritarian distribution operates according to a different political logic than democratic distribution, it would be hard to find better evidence than any suggesting that ethnic polarization tends to inspire distribution in autocracies as systematically as it dampens distribution in democracies.

comprehensive forms of distribution. This kind of coexistence of ethnocracy with robust distributive politics is hardly limited to East Asia. Jordan, with its cleaved political economy between Transjordanians controlling the state and public sector and Palestinians dominating the commercial economy, is another seminal case in point. We are grateful to Sean Yom for suggesting this example.

References

Acemoglu, Daron, and James Robinson. 2006. *Economic Origins of Dictatorship and Democracy*. Cambridge: Cambridge University Press.

Albertus, Michael. 2015. *Autocracy and Redistribution: The Politics of Land Reform*. New York: Cambridge University Press.

Alberto Diaz-Cayeros, Beatriz Magaloni, and Barry Weingast. 2016. "Authoritarian Survival and Poverty Traps: Land Reform in Mexico." *World Development* 77: 154–170.

and Oliver Kaplan. 2013. "Land Reform as a Counterinsurgency Policy: Evidence from Colombia." *Journal of Conflict Resolution* 57(2): 198–231.

and Victor Menaldo. 2012. "If You're Against Them You're With Us: The Effect of Expropriation on Autocratic Survival." *Comparative Political Studies* 45 (8): 973–1003.

and Victor Menaldo. 2014. "Gaming Democracy: Elite Dominance during Transition and the Prospects for Redistribution." *British Journal of Political Science* 44 (3): 575–603.

Thomas Brambor, and Ricardo Ceneviva. 2018. "Land Inequality and Rural Unrest: Theory and Evidence from Brazil." *Journal of Conflict Resolution* 62(3): 557–596.

Alesina, Alberto, and Dani Rodrik. 1994. "Distributive Politics and Economic Growth." *Quarterly Journal of Economics* 109: 465–90.

and Eliana La Ferrara. 2004. "Ethnic Diversity and Economic Performance." *National Bureau of Economic Research Working Paper Series*, no. 10313.

Alvarez, José. 2004. *Cuba's Agricultural Sector*. Gainesville: University Press of Florida.

Amemiya, Takeshi. 1973. "Regression Analysis When the Dependent Variable Is Truncated Normal." *Econometrica* 41(6): 997–1016.

Atkinson, Anthony. 2015. *Inequality*. Cambridge, MA: Harvard University Press.

Ayubi, Nazih N. M. 1982. "Bureaucratic Inflation and Administrative Inefficiency: The Deadlock in Egyptian Administration." *Middle Eastern Studies* 18(3): 286–299.

Baland, Jean Marie, and James Robinson. 2008. "Land and Power: Theory and Evidence from Chile." *American Economic Review* 98(5): 1737–1765.

Barro, Robert, and Xavier Sala-i-Martin. 1995. *Economic Growth.* New York: McGraw Hill.

Bartels, Larry. 2005. "Homer Gets a Tax Cut: Inequality and Public Policy in the American Mind." *Perspectives on Politics* 3(1): 15–31.

Bennett, Andrew and Jeffrey Checkel, eds. 2014. *Process Tracing: From Metaphor to Analytic Tool.* Cambridge: Cambridge University Press.

Berry, Albert, and William Cline. 1979. *Agrarian Structure and Productivity in Developing Countries.* Baltimore, MD: Johns Hopkins University Press.

Besley, Timothy, and Robin Burgess. 2000. "Land Reform, Poverty Reduction, and Growth: Evidence from India." *Quarterly Journal of Economics* 115(2): 389–430.

Bianchi, Robert. 1989. *Unruly Corporatism: Associational Life in Twentieth-Century Egypt.* New York: Oxford University Press.

Blaydes, Lisa. 2010. *Elections and Distributive Politics in Mubarak's Egypt.* Cambridge: Cambridge University Press.

Boix, Carles. 2003. *Democracy and Redistribution.* Cambridge: Cambridge University Press.

Michael Miller, and Sebastian Rosato. 2013. "A Complete Dataset of Political Regimes, 1800–2007." *Comparative Political Studies* 46(12): 1523–1554.

Bräutigam, Deborah. 1994. "What Can Africa Learn from Taiwan? Political Economy, Industrial Policy, and Adjustment." *The Journal of Modern African Studies* 32(1): 111–138.

Brownlee, Jason. 2007. *Authoritarianism in an Age of Democratization.* New York: Cambridge University Press.

Bueno de Mesquita, Bruce, Alastair Smith, Randolph M. Siverson, and James D. Morrow. 2003. *The Logic of Political Survival.* Boston, MA: MIT Press.

Burn, Melissa M. 2006. "Loyalty and Order: Clan Identity and Political Preference in Kyrgyzstan and Kazakhstan, 2005." PhD Dissertation, George Mason University, Fairfax, VA.

Cheibub, José Antonio, Jennifer Gandhi, and James Raymond Vreeland. 2010. "Democracy and Dictatorship Revisited." *Public Choice* 143(1–2): 67–101.

Coatsworth, John. 2008. "Inequality, Institutions and Economic Growth in Latin America." *Journal of Latin American Studies* 40(3): 545–569.

Cockcroft, James. 1983. *Mexico: Class Formation, Capital Accumulation and the State*. New York: Monthly Review Press.

Collins, Kathleen. 2002. "Clans, Pacts, and Politics in Central Asia." *Journal of Democracy* 13(3): 137–152.

Cornelius, Wayne. 1975. *Politics and the Migrant Poor in Mexico City*. Stanford: Stanford University Press.

Crouch, Harold. 1996. *Government and Society in Malaysia*. Ithaca, NY: Cornell University Press.

Crystal, Jill. 1990. *Oil and Politics in the Gulf: Rulers and Merchants in Kuwait and Qatar*. Cambridge: Cambridge University Press.

de Alcántara, Cynthia. 1976. *Modernizing Mexican Agriculture: Socioeconomic Implications of Technological Change, 1940-1970*. Geneva, Switzerland: United Nations Research Institute for Social Development.

Deeb, Marius. 1979. *Party Politics in Egypt: The Wafd and Its Rivals, 1919–1939*. Ithaca, NY: Ithaca Press.

de Janvry, Alain. 1981. *The Agrarian Question and Reformism in Latin America*. Baltimore, MD: Johns Hopkins University Press.

Marco Gonzalez-Navarro, and Elisabeth Sadoulet. 2014. "Are Land Reforms Granting Complete Property Rights Politically Risky? Electoral Outcomes of Mexico's Certification Program." *Journal of Development Economics* 110: 216–225.

De Soto, Hernando. 2000. *The Mystery of Capital: Why Capitalism Triumphs in the West and Fails Everywhere Else*. New York: Basic Books.

Deininger, Klaus. 2003. "Land Policies for Growth and Poverty Reduction." Washington, DC: World Bank.

and Juan Sebastian Chamorro. 2004. "Investment and Equity Effects of Land Regularisation: The Case of Nicaragua." *Agricultural Economics* 30(2): 101–116.

Daniel Ayalew Ali, and Takashi Yamano. 2008. "Legal Knowledge and Economic Development: The Case of Land Rights in Uganda." *Land Economics* 84(4): 593–619.

Demsetz, Harold. 1967. "Toward a Theory of Property Rights." *American Economic Review* 57(2): 347–359.

Dickson, Bruce. 1993. "The Lessons of Defeat: The Reorganization of the Kuomintang on Taiwan, 1950–52." *The China Quarterly* 133: 56–84.

Doner, Richard, Bryan Ritchie, and Dan Slater. 2005. "Systemic Vulnerability and the Origins of Developmental States: Northeast and Southeast Asia in Comparative Perspective." *International Organization* 59(2): 327–361.

Domínguez, Jorge. 1978. *Cuba: Order and Revolution.* Cambridge, MA: Harvard University Press.

Easterly, William. 2001. "Can Institutions Resolve Ethnic Conflict?" *Economic Development and Cultural Change* 49(4): 687–706.

and Ross Levine. 1997. "Africa's Growth Tragedy: Policies and Ethnic Divisions." *Quarterly Journal of Economics* 112(4): 1203–1250.

Eckstein, Salomón. 1968. *El Marco Macroeconómico del Problema Agrario Mexicano.* Mexico: Centro de Investigaciones Agrarias.

El-Ghobashy, Mona. 2011. "The Praxis of the Egyptian Revolution." *Middle East Report* 41(258): 2–13.

Engerman, Stanley, and Kenneth Sokoloff. 2002. "Factor Endowments, Inequality, and Paths of Development Among New World Economies." *National Bureau of Economic Research Working Paper,* No. 9259.

Feder, Gershon, and David Feeny. 1991. "Land Tenure and Property Rights: Theory and Implications for Development Policy." *World Bank Economic Review* 5(1): 135–153.

Fenner, Sofia. 2016. "Life after Co-optation." PhD dissertation, The University of Chicago, Chicago, IL.

Fu, Diana. 2018. *Mobilizing Without the Masses: Control and Contention in China.* New York: Cambridge University Press.

Furnivall, John. 1948. *Colonial Policy and Practice: A Comparative Study of Burma and Netherlands India.* New York: New York University Press.

Galor, Oded, Omer Moav, and Dietrich Vollrath. 2009. "Inequality in Landownership, the Emergence of Human-Capital Promoting Institutions, and the Great Divergence." *Review of Economic Studies* 76(1): 143–179.

Gandhi, Jennifer, and Adam Przeworski. 2007. "Authoritarian Institutions and the Survival of Autocrats." *Comparative Political Studies* **40**(11): 1279–1301.

George, Cherian. 2000. *Singapore: The Air-Conditioned Nation.* Singapore: Landmark Books.

Gilens, Martin, and Benjamin Page. 2014. "Testing Theories of American Politics: Elites, Interest Groups, and Average Citizens." *Perspectives on Politics* 12(3): 564–581.

Goldstein, Markus, and Christopher Udry. 2008. "The Profits of Power: Land Rights and Agricultural Investment in Ghana." *Journal of Political Economy* 116(6): 981–1022.

Goemans, Hein, Kristian Skrede Gleditsch, and Giacomo Chiozza. 2009. "Introducing Archigos: A Dataset of Political Leaders." Journal of Peace Research 46(2): 269–283.

Gordon, Joel. 1989. "The False Hopes of 1950: The Wafd's Last Hurrah and the Demise of Egypt's Old Order." *International Journal of Middle East Studies* 21(2): 193–214.

Hack, Karl. 1999. "The Malayan Emergency: The Role of Special Branch and Intelligence." Working Paper, Institute for Southeast Asian Studies, Singapore.

Haggard, Stephan, and Robert R. Kaufman. 1995. *The Political Economy of Democratic Transitions.* Princeton, NJ: Princeton University Press.

Hay, Rupert. 1955. "The Impact of the Oil Industry on the Persian Gulf Shaykhdoms." *Middle East Journal* 9: 361–372.

Hightower, Victoria P. 2013. "Pearling and Political Power in the Trucial States, 1850–1930: Debts, Taxes, and Politics." *Journal of Arabian Studies* 3(2): 215–231.

Hsiau, A-Chin. 1997. "Language Ideology in Taiwan: The KMT's Language Policy, the Tai-Yu Language Movement, and Ethnic Politics." *Journal of Multilingual and Multicultural Development* 18(4): 302–315.

Hopper, Matthew S. 2015. *Slaves of One Master: Globalization and Slavery in Arabia in the Age of Empire.* New Haven, CT: Yale University Press.

Huntington, Samuel. 1968. *Political Order in Changing Societies.* New Haven, CT: Yale University Press.

Ismail, Salwa. 2013. "Urban Subalterns in the Arab Revolutions: Cairo and Damascus in Comparative Perspective." *Comparative Studies in Society and History* 55(4): 865–894.

2006. *Political Life in Cairo's New Quarters: Encountering the Everyday State.* Minneapolis: University of Minnesota Press.

Kassem, May. 1999. *In the Guise of Democracy: Governance in Contemporary Egypt.* Reading, NY: Ithaca Press.

Koo, Anthony. 1966. "Economic Consequences of Land Reform in Taiwan." *Asian Survey* 6(3): 150–157.

Kourí, Emilio. 2015, January. "La invención del ejido." *Nexos*.

Kuhonta, Erik Martinez. 2011. *The Institutional Imperative: The Politics of Equitable Development in Southeast Asia*. Stanford, CA: Stanford University Press.

Kuo, Shirley, John Fei, and Gustav Ranis. 1981. *The Taiwan Success Story*. Boulder, CO: Westview Press.

Lapp, Nancy. 2004. *Landing Votes: Representation and Land Reform in Latin America*. New York: Palgrave Macmillan.

Lee, Ching Kwan. 2007. *Against the Law: Labor Protests in China's Rustbelt and Sunbelt*. Berkeley: University of California Press.

Levinson, Jerome, and Juan de Onís. 1970. *The Alliance That Lost Its Way: A Critical Report on the Alliance for Progress*. Chicago, IL: Quadrangle Books.

Loh, Kah Seng. 2013. *Squatters into Citizens: The 1961 Bukit Ho Swee Fire and the Making of Modern Singapore*. Honolulu, HI: Asian Studies Association of Australia.

Lorimer, John Gordon. 1915. *Gazeteer of the Persian Gulf, 'Oman, and Central Arabia*, vol. II. Calcutta: Superintendent Government Printing.

Lust, Ellen. 2009. "Competitive Clientelism in the Middle East." *Journal of Democracy* 20(3): 122–35.

Magaloni, Beatriz. 2006. *Voting for Autocracy*. New York: Cambridge University Press.

Mainwaring, Scott, Daniel Brinks, and Aníbal Pérez-Liñán. 2001. "Classifying Political Regimes in Latin." *Studies in Comparative International Development* 36(1): 37–65.

Mardini, Zuhayr. 1984. *Al-ladudan: al-wafd wa-l-ikhwan*. Beirut: Dar Iqra'.

Matsuzaki, Reo. 2012. "Institutions by Imposition: Colonial Lessons for Contemporary State-Building." PhD Dissertation, Massachusetts Institute of Technology.

Mauzy, Diane and R. S. Milne. 2002. *Singapore Politics Under the People's Action Party*. London: Routledge.

Mears, Leon. 1962. "Agriculture and Food Situation in Cuba." Economic Research Service, No. 28.

Meltzer, Allan, and Scott Richard. 1981. "A Rational Theory of the Size of Government." *Journal of Political Economy* 89: 914–27.

Migdal, Joel. 1988. *Strong Societies and Weak States*. Princeton, NJ: Princeton University Press.

Mitchell, Timothy. 2002. *Rule of Experts: Egypt, Techno-politics, Modernity*. Berkeley: University of California Press.

1998. "The Market's Place," in Nicholas S. Hopkins and Kirsten Westergaard, eds., *Directions of Change in Rural Egypt*. Cairo: The American University in Cairo Press, 19–40.

1991. "The Limits of the State: Beyond Statist Approaches and Their Critics." *The American Political Science Review* 85(1): 77–96.

Montalvo, Jose, and Marta Reynal-Querol. 2005. "Ethnic Polarization, Potential Conflict, and Civil Wars." *American Economic Review* 95 (3): 796–816.

Morrow, James, Bruce Bueno de Mesquita, Randolph Siverson, and Alastair Smith. 2008. "Retesting Selectorate Theory: Separating the Effects of W from Other Elements of Democracy." *American Political Science Review* 102(3): 393–400.

Moore Jr., Barrington. 1966. *Social Origins of Dictatorship and Democracy: Lord and Peasant in the Making of the Modern World*. Boston, MA: Beacon Press.

Myers, Ramon. 2009. "Towards an Enlightened Authoritarian Polity: The Kuomintang Central Reform Committee on Taiwan, 1950–1952." *Journal of Contemporary China* 18(59): 185–199.

North, Douglass, and Robert Thomas. 1973. *The Rise of the Western World: A New Economic History*. New York: Cambridge University Press.

O'Connor, James. 1968. "Agrarian Reforms in Cuba, 1958–1963." *Science and Society* 32(2): 169–217.

Ostrom, Elinor. 1990. *Governing the Commons*. New York: Cambridge University Press.

Ostwald, Kai, and Guillem Riambau. 2017. "Voting Behavior When Votes are Potentially Traceable." Paper presented at Annual Meetings of the Western Political Science Association, Vancouver, April.

Otero, Gerardo. 1989. "Agrarian Reform in Mexico: Capitalism and the State." In William Thiesenhusen, ed. *Searching for Agrarian Reform in Latin America*. Boston: Unwin Hyman, 276–304.

Palazuelos, Enrique and Rafael Fernandez. 2012. "Kazakhstan: Oil Endowment and Oil Empowerment." *Communist and Post-Communist Studies* 45(1–2): 27–37.

Pepinsky, Thomas. 2009. *Economic Crises and the Breakdown of Authoritarian Regimes: Indonesia and Malaysia in Comparative Perspective.* New York: Cambridge University Press.

Perry, Elizabeth. 1997. "From Native Place to Workplace: Labor Origins and Outcomes of China's Danwei System." In Xiaobu Lu and Elizabeth Perry (eds.), *Danwei: The Changing Chinese Workplace in Historical and Comparative Perspective.* New York: M. E. Sharpe.

Persson, Torsten, and Guido Tabellini. 2002. *Political Economics: Explaining Economic Policy.* Cambridge, MA: MIT Press.

Posusney, Marsha Pripstein. 1997. *Labor and the State in Egypt: Workers, Unions, and Economic Restructuring.* New York: Columbia University Press.

Rajan, Raghuram, and Luigi Zingales. 2003. "The Great Reversals: The Politics of Financial Development in the Twentieth Century." *Journal of Financial Economics* 69(1): 5-50.

and Rodney Ramcharan. 2011. "Land and Credit: A Study of the Political Economy of Banking in the United States in the Early 20th Century." *Journal of Finance* 66(6): 1895-1931.

Read, Benjamin L. 2012. *Roots of the State: Neighborhood Organization and Social Networks in Beijing and Taipei.* Stanford, CA: Stanford University Press.

Rodan, Garry. 1996. "State-Society Relations and Political Opposition in Singapore." In Garry Rodan (ed.), *Political Oppositions in Industrializing Asia.* London: Routledge.

Rodrik, Dani. 1995. "Getting Interventions Right: How South Korea and Taiwan Grew Rich." *Economic Policy* 10(20): 53-107.

Roemer, John. 1998. "Why the Poor Do Not Expropriate the Rich: An Old Argument in New Garb." *Journal of Public Economics* 70(3): 399-424.

Ross, Michael L. 2001. "Does Oil Hinder Democracy?" *World Politics* 53 (3): 325-361.

Saab, Gabriel S. 1967. *The Egyptian Agrarian Reform: 1952-1962.* London: Oxford University Press.

Sanderson, Steven. 1986. *The Transformation of Mexican Agriculture.* Princeton: Princeton University Press.

Sanderson, Susan R. Walsh. 1984. *Land Reform in Mexico: 1910—1980.* Orlando, FL: Academic Press.

Saulniers, Alfred. 1988. *Public Enterprises in Peru: Public Sector Growth and Reform.* Boulder, CO: Westview Press.

Schatz, Edward. 2004. Modern Clan Politics: The Power of "Blood" in Kazakhstan and Beyond. Seattle: University of Washington Press.

Shiau, Chyuan-jeng. 1984. "The Political Economy of Rice Policies in Taiwan, 1945-1980." PhD Dissertation, University of Pennsylvania.

Skocpol, Theda and Margaret Somers. 1980. "The Uses of Comparative History in Macrosocial Inquiry." *Comparative Studies in Society and History* 22(2): 174-197.

Scott, James C. 1999. *Seeing Like a State: How Certain Schemes to Improve the Human Condition Have Failed*. New Haven, CT: Yale University Press.

  1985. *Weapons of the Weak: Everyday Forms of Peasant Resistance*. New Haven, CT: Yale University Press.

Seragaldin, Samia. 2000. *The Cairo House: A Novel*. Syracuse, NY: Syracuse University Press.

Shapiro, Ian. 2002. "Why the Poor Don't Soak the Rich." *Daedalus* 131(1): 118-128.

Simmons, Erica and Nicholas Rush Smith. 2017. "Comparison with an Ethnographic Sensibility." *PS: Political Science and Politics* 50(1): 126-130.

Sims, David. 2010. *Understanding Cairo: Logic of a City Out of Control*. Cairo: The American University in Cairo Press.

Singh, Prerna and Matthias vom Hau. 2016. "Ethnicity in Time: Politics, History, and the Relationship between Ethnic Diversity and Public Goods Provision." *Comparative Political Studies* 49(10): 1303-1340.

Slater, Dan. 2010. *Ordering Power: Contentious Politics and Authoritarian Leviathans in Southeast Asia*. New York: Cambridge University Press.

  and Sofia Fenner. 2011. "State Power and Staying Power: Infrastructural Mechanisms and Authoritarian Durability." *Journal of International Affairs* 65(1): 15-29.

  and Joseph Wong. 2013. "The Strength to Concede: Ruling Parties and Democratization in Developmental Asia." *Perspectives on Politics* 11 (3): 717-733.

  and Daniel Ziblatt. 2013. "The Enduring Indispensability of the Controlled Comparison." *Comparative Political Studies* 46(10): 1301-1327.

Solinger, Dorothy. 1999. *Contesting Citizenship in Urban China: Peasant Migrants, the State, and the Logic of the Market*. Berkeley: University of California Press.

Sonbol, Amira El Azhary. 2000. *The New Mamluks: Egyptian Society and Modern Feudalism*. Syracuse, NY: Syracuse University Press.

Stokes, Susan C., Thad Dunning, Marcelo Nazareno, and Valeria Brusco. 2013. *Brokers, Voters, and Clientelism: The Puzzle of Distributive Politics*. New York: Cambridge University Press.

Svolik, Milan. 2012. *The Politics of Authoritarian Rule*. New York: Cambridge University Press.

Tai, Hung-Chao. 1974. *Land Reform and Politics*. Berkeley: University of California Press.

Themnér, Lotta, and Peter Wallensteen. 2013. "Armed Conflict, 1946-2012." *Journal of Peace Research* 50(4): 509-521.

Thiesenhusen, William, ed. 1989. *Searching for Agrarian Reform in Latin America*. Boston, MA: Unwin Hyman.

1995. *Broken Promises: Agrarian Reform and the Latin American Campesino*. Boulder, CO: Westview Press.

Thomas, Hugh. 1971. *Cuba: The Pursuit of Freedom*. New York: Harper & Row.

Trocki, Carl. 2006. *Singapore: Wealth, Power, and the Culture of Control*. New York: Routledge.

United States Energy Information Administration. 2017. "Country Analysis Brief: Kazakhstan." Available at www.ieee.es/en/Galerias/fichero/OtrasPublicaciones/Internacional/2017/EIA_Country_Aanlysis_Kazakhstan_10may2017.pdf.

Valdés Paz, Juan. 1997. *Procesos Agrarios en Cuba, 1959-1995*. La Habana: Editorial de Ciencias Sociales.

Vanhanen, Tatu. 2009. Index of Power Resources (IPR) 2007. FSD2420, version 1.0. Tampere: Finnish Social Science Data Archive.

Vu, Tuong. 2010. *Paths to Development in Asia: South Korea, Vietnam, China, and Indonesia*. New York: Cambridge University Press.

Waldner, David. 1999. *State Building and Late Development*. Ithaca, NY: Cornell University Press.

Wallace, Jeremy. 2014. *Cities and Stability: Urbanization, Redistribution, and Regime Survival in China*. New York: Oxford University Press.

Walsh, Katherine. 2012. "Putting Inequality in Its Place: Rural Consciousness and the Power of Perspective." *American Political Science Review* 1(1): 1-16.

Walsh Sanderson, Susan. 1984. *Land Reform in Mexico: 1910-1980*. Orlando, FL: Academic Press.

Warriner, Doreen. 1962. *Land Reform and Development in the Middle East: A Study of Egypt, Syria, and Iraq*, 2nd ed. New York: Oxford University Press.

Wedeen, Lisa. 1999. *Ambiguities of Domination: Politics, Rhetoric, and Symbols in Contemporary Syria*. Chicago, IL: University of Chicago Press.

Woodward, Susan. 1995. *Balkan Tragedy: Chaos and Dissolution after the Cold War*. Washington, DC: Brookings Institution Press.

Yom, Sean. 2015. *From Resilience to Revolution: How Foreign Interventions Destabilize the Middle East*. New York: Columbia University Press.

Zahlan, Rosemarie Said. 1989. *The Making of the Modern Gulf States: Kuwait, Bahrain, Qatar, the United Arab Emirates and Oman*. London: Routledge.

Cambridge Elements ≡

Politics of Development

Elements in the series

Developmental States
Stephan Haggard
9781108449496

Coercive Distribution
Michael Albertus, Sofia Fenner and Dan Slater
9781108462136

A full series listing is available at: www.cambridge.org/EPOD

Printed in the United States
By Bookmasters